Advance Praise for *The Mediator's Handbook*

Can you really make the classic book in its field even better? In this book, authors Jennifer Beer and Caroline Packard prove that, when it comes to mediation, the answer is a resounding "Yes!" This new edition of *The Mediator's Handbook* provides new tools, new scripts, and new frameworks that will assist experienced practitioners and novices alike. Based on up-to-date research foundations from anthropology, psychology, and behavioral neuroscience, the authors take us by the hand and lead us step-by-step through the mediation process, suggesting concrete strategies to help people in conflict work through difficult emotions to actionable ideas for resolving their disputes. Bravo!

— G. Richard Shell, Thomas Gerrity Professor of Legal Studies and Business Ethics at the Wharton School of Business and author of *Bargaining for Advantage: Negotiation Strategies for Reasonable People*

The fourth edition of *The Mediator's Handbook* continues to improve upon everything that made the original edition a success: user-friendly explanations for every step of the mediation process, starting with what mediation is, to dealing with the most difficult situations that can arise in the course of a dispute. While the *Handbook* presents itself as being for mediators, those who should have a copy of the *Handbook* on their shelf include lawyers representing clients in litigation, human resources executives, managers of complex international infrastructure projects, or school counselors dealing with difficult teenagers. In short, *The Mediator's Handbook* is a comprehensive and practical guide for anyone who regularly deals with conflict.

— Michael McIlwrath, co-author of *International Arbitration and Mediation: A Practical Guide*, and host of the podcast "International Dispute Negotiation"

Plenty of mediation books will give you the kind of language ordinary mediators use – the same language we are used to hearing from other helping professions, such as lawyers, and therapists. What these authors let us in on – is the secret language of outstanding mediators. They generously share hundreds of examples of carefully chosen phrases mediators can use at every step that make the difference between knowing what needs to happen next in mediation, and being able to make it happen.

— Hideaki Irei, Associate Professor, Faculty of Law, Kyushu University

The Mediator's Handbook is the basic primer for anyone who is seriously interested in resolving conflicts constructively. I have used it in my classroom for the last twenty years. This new edition gives us even more insights and practical suggestions for how to deal with the complexity of disputes in many different kinds of situations. Beer, Packard and Stief are masters in the mediation field and have much to offer us. An essential addition to the current scholarship and practice.

— Susan Sgorbati, Jones Chair for Social Activism,
and former Dean of Faculty, Bennington College

The Mediator's Handbook continues to be solid, and speaks to the needs of the participants.

— Mohammed Abu-Nimer, Ph.D., International Peace and Conflict Resolution,
School of International Service, American University

THE MEDIATOR'S HANDBOOK

REVISED & EXPANDED FOURTH EDITION

JENNIFER E. BEER & CAROLINE C. PACKARD

with Eileen Stief

new society
PUBLISHERS

ISBN: 978-0-86571-722-0
eISBN: 978-1-55092-516-6

Book design: Gregory Green and John McKercher with Jennifer Beer.
Illustrations: Elizabeth Elwood Gates, Jennifer Beer

LIBRARY AND ARCHIVES CANADA CATALOGUING IN PUBLICATION

Beer, Jennifer E.
The mediator's handbook / Jennifer E. Beer & Caroline
C. Packard ; with Eileen Stief. — Rev. and expanded 4th ed.

Includes index.
ISBN 978-0-86571-722-0

1. Conflict management.   2. Mediation.   3. Negotiation.
4. Interpersonal conflict.   I. Packard, Caroline C.
II. Stief, Eileen   III. Title.

BF637.I48B33 2012   303.6'9   C2012-903793-1

New Society Publishers' mission is to publish books that contribute in fundamental ways to building an ecologically sustainable and just society, and to do so with the least possible impact on the environment, in a manner that models this vision. We are committed to doing this not just through education, but through action. The interior pages of our bound books are printed on Forest Stewardship Council®-registered acid-free paper that is **100% post-consumer recycled** (100% old growth forest-free), processed chlorine free, and printed with vegetable-based, low-VOC inks, with covers produced using FSC®-registered stock. New Society also works to reduce its carbon footprint, and purchases carbon offsets based on an annual audit to ensure a carbon neutral footprint. For further information, or to browse our full list of books and purchase securely, visit our website at: **www.newsociety.com**

***THE MEDIATOR'S HANDBOOK* ONLINE**

Want more details? To keep *The Mediator's Handbook* portable, we have put additional topics and resources online at mediatorshandbook.com, including materials for teachers and trainers.

RECYCLED
Paper made from
recycled material
FSC® C103567

Printed in Canada

Table of Contents

Welcome to the 4th edition of *The Mediator's Handbook*!

Who hasn't found themselves between people who are in a bitter fight...and wanted to do SOMETHING constructive about it?

Maybe you picked up this book because you're already a mediator. Maybe you're studying conflict resolution in a class, or taking mediation training. Maybe your job often puts you in the midst of other people's conflicts.

Whether you are new to mediation and need a clear map to follow, or a professional seeking to improve your negotiation and conflict management skills, or a long-time mediator and trainer looking for new ideas and coherent frameworks, *The Mediator's Handbook* is designed to be an ongoing resource for you.

What's in the book?

The *Handbook* focuses on round-the-table mediations with up to about eight participants, where the mediators primarily facilitate discussion and decisions to meet participants' goals for the mediation, rather than steering them toward settlement terms or relationship repair. This book's process and skills also provide a solid platform for the additional methods and knowledge needed to mediate larger-scale conflicts. After the **Overview** chapter helps you get your bearings, the next three chapters lay out the anatomy of our basic mediation process:

- **Getting to the Table** — setting up a mediation.

- **Exploring the Situation** — a step-by-step look at the first half of the mediation, which is mostly an open discussion of their concerns.

- **Reaching Resolution** — the problem-solving and planning phases.

Each phase is presented with a purpose, steps, tasks, and examples.

The mediation structure may seem simple, even obvious, yet it rests on a host of skills that can take a while to internalize. The book's second half, the Toolbox, has four chapters that address the main concepts and skill sets mediators need:

- **Understanding Conflict**

- **Supporting the People**

- **Facilitating the Process**

- **Solving the Problem**

The basic structure and the skill sets adapt well to different types of conflicts, from formal interventions in large disputes, to informal meetings where no one realizes they are participating in a "mediation." In this spirit, the final chapter, "**Going Further**," looks at evaluation, adaptation, and resources.

What's new?

To update the *Handbook*, three of us — Jenny Beer, Caroline Packard, Joan Broadfield — met regularly for more than two years. It turned out we knew a lot more than we did 17 years ago when Jenny wrote the previous edition with Eileen Stief. For every page, we compared mediation experiences, training strategies, and academic theories. We argued, scrapped cherished notions, read books and blogs, then tried again, because we wanted to bring you the most reliable and understandable information we could.

Long-time readers (thank you!) will find this new edition much changed. There are new terms, lots more how-to examples, and clearer ways to decide, "What should I be doing now?" These rest on a coherent and tested framework for understanding what works in mediation and why. We think you will like it, but just in case, you'll also find some of the beloved 3rd edition pages on our **mediatorshandbook.com** website, plus more resources and "outtakes" from this 4th edition.

The final pages of this book describe the authors' backgrounds, and thank a few of the many people who have contributed to this project. Though *The Mediator's Handbook* and our mediating lives are no longer officially connected to Quakers, we greatly appreciate Philadelphia Yearly Meeting's steadfast support of mediation and *The Mediator's Handbook* over many decades. It has enriched the content of this new edition in more ways than we can count.

Take it with you

The field of mediation has expanded dramatically since Philadelphia Quakers put together the first *Mediator's Handbook* in 1982. Formal conflict resolution processes have since become part of our everyday landscape. Mediation is now a full-blown profession. We have expanded out from neighbor and family conflicts to divorce and custody disputes, and conflicts in businesses, organizations, and communities.

Though professional mediators offer valuable experience and a large set of facilitation tools, in real life, most conflicts are mediated by trusted people who are near at hand. For decades, *The Mediator's Handbook* has empowered a wide range of people — wherever they find themselves — to help people talk through their differences, ease hard feelings, and find their own constructive solutions to the difficulties in their lives. To all those peacemakers, and to each of you, we offer this new edition in the hope that you will go out and use it often.

— JEB, CCP, JGB
March 2012

OVERVIEW

1

What is mediation?

▶ Mediation is...

✓ A process

✓ for resolving disputes

✓ where an intermediary helps

✓ conflicting parties

✓ have a conversation

✓ to jointly resolve their concerns.

Process: Mediation follows an organic sequence that unfolds differently in each situation, but still has recognizable phases.

Disputes: Usually parties have specific incidents, disagreements, and concerns that have brought them to mediation, things they want changed. The mediation may also address underlying conflicts and systemic causes, if the parties want to take on that larger project.

Intermediary: Literally, "one who goes between," by definition a mediator has some degree of impartiality and detachment from the outcome. Mediators guide the process; however, *the parties* do the work of coming up with the solutions and making the decisions.

Parties: These may be a person, a group, or a whole nation—who come as a unit to the mediation, or are represented there, and who share a common identity or interests.

Conversation: The way out of conflict is through dialogue, which means talking and listening directly to each other. Dialogue broadens the parties' understanding of their situation, of each other, and of their desired future. This is rarely a neat or rational process!

Jointly resolve concerns: The goal is workable, durable solutions that meet the participants' practical, emotional, and social concerns as fully as possible. Mediators work to create a cooperative atmosphere for problem-solving where the parties themselves plan how they wish to proceed, individually and collectively.

There are many kinds of conflict, and, increasingly, many kinds of mediation. This definition reflects the type of conflicts that are the focus of this book—interpersonal disputes where parties have some ongoing connection—and the principles and methods we have developed through mediating them.

SAMPLE SITUATIONS

➤ Tom's Toys has not yet paid for a major re-wiring job because they claim the work was not finished properly. The electrician, Morgan, hotly denies this, saying that Tom is just inventing excuses not to pay because his business is doing poorly. After three months, Morgan contacts a small-business media-tor, hoping to deal with the matter quietly and not take it to court.

➤ The governing board of GoodWorks is split between its visionary founder and the new chair of the board. The group is trying to set up a mediation between the two leaders, before a consultant works with the larger board.

A useful tool

SAMPLE SITUATION

➤ CrossCurrent City Council is battling their private volunteer fire company over access to the company's account books and budget. The 110-year-old company, mostly men from "old-timer" families, is proud of its independence and doesn't want "new-comer" bureaucrats snooping or managing their affairs. Three firefighters meet with two council members to forge compromise legislation.

▶ Mending fences: Practical solutions, emotional resolutions

Mediation can work spectacularly well. People find solutions to thorny problems. They let go of their sense of grievance and mend broken relationships. In most mediations, people get some emotional relief, and walk away with a plan that resolves most of their concerns.

There are no guarantees, of course—though most mediations work out, some don't. Mediators may sense that the parties are making grudging compromises that are unlikely to last. Or the parties may quit the mediation, still feeling angry or discouraged. However, even when there's no agreement, the emotional charge of the dispute may lessen once people have had their say. And participants can at least walk away with a more informed and realistic picture of their situation, and make their next decisions from that vantage point.

▶ Building stronger organizations and communities

Mediation is a time-tested choice in an ever-growing array of conflict intervention methods—from formal and public litigation, to peace-building projects, to quiet backstage coaching. Mediation techniques can also amplify the success of other approaches, such as negotiation, advocacy, arbitration, meeting facilitation, or training initiatives. For instance, a politician might mediate a local water-rights issue as part of postwar peace building. Corporations often proceed with litigation until they collect enough information to submit a dispute to mediation. If a volcanic argument between two key players disrupts a planning conference, the facilitator might ask them to meet for a mediated conversation before the next day's session.

In a broader context, mediation offers people a way to take charge of their own conflicts and solutions. Mediation processes (or even just the skills) can help communities and organizations survive their conflicts and benefit from them. Mediation can strengthen working relationships and alliances. At its best, mediation strengthens democratic, collaborative efforts to meet people's needs more effectively.

What makes mediation work?

▶ Why it works

New mediators are often amazed to see how one or two mediation sessions can turn around long-standing conflicts. What makes mediation so effective?

It starts and ends with what the participants care about

➤ Mediation takes seriously the issues that people say matter most to them — relationships, fairness, emotions, justice, recognition, respect, inclusion, fixing a problem.

➤ People get a chance to tell each other their frustrations and hurts, to express regret, and to ask for what they need.

➤ Parties can bring up whatever topics concern them — they are not restricted to resolving only the official complaint.

Mediation provides structure for difficult conversations

➤ It's a private and supportive setting for checking out misunderstandings and suspicions, and for speaking honestly.

➤ Mediators explore and reframe the parties' interests in ways that help people move into problem-solving mode.

➤ A mediated agreement can lessen subsequent friction and misunderstandings, even if the conflict is not fully resolved.

▶ Mediation works best when…

✓ Parties realize that continuing their dispute may have costly consequences.

✓ They genuinely want to change the situation and need each other's cooperation to do so.

✓ All main stakeholders and decision-makers participate.

✓ The parties are (eventually) able to express the reasons for their discomfort and distress.

✓ The parties are capable of making plans and keeping promises.

If someone is bent on keeping a conflict going or winning outright, even the most obvious solutions are not likely to work. If everyone is ready to end a conflict, mediation can be a graceful and efficient way to do so.

1.3 SAMPLE SITUATIONS

➤ Henry is frail and a bit forgetful. After months of acrimony and denial, his three children, several grandchildren, plus Henry are meeting with a mediator to work out an agreement detailing who should handle Henry's money, who will find him an appropriate nursing home, and who will clean out and sell the family house. (See page 171 for an agreement they might have reached.)

➤ The neighbors of a movie theater have complained about loud music, parking in front of their houses, and people loitering late at night. Following a disturbing incident of vandalism, the manager asked a mediator to facilitate a meeting of the neighbors.

The mediator's role

1.4
THE SATISFACTIONS OF MEDIATING

Mediators speak about the challenges and satisfactions of mediating:

"People get discouraged… You have doubts too, but it is important to say, 'Yes, you are getting somewhere. You are talking.' It is a miracle to see at the end of the session how it has come together."

"The simplicity of it is almost embarrassing. In two hours, people can solve 'impossible' problems and let out hostility which has sometimes built up for years. The exciting part of mediating is watching that process work again and again for different people in different situations."

▶ Mediators guide but don't decide

Mediators have little or no stake in the conflict or the terms of its resolution, in the model we use. Rather than advocating for one party's benefit, they help the parties work towards an outcome that best satisfies everyone. Participants may not know the mediator at all, or they may be closely connected. What's important is that the mediator be someone all the parties trust enough to allow the intervention and to speak freely about their concerns.

Mediators are in charge of the process, and provide two essential ingredients:

➤ **A structure for conversation** to help people talk, listen, and think.

➤ **Caring, impartial attentiveness** to people, process, and concerns.

▶ Who can mediate?

Mediation isn't esoteric. People have been mediating for as long as people have been fighting, and most adults have picked up some mediation skills along the way. This means people from all walks of life and with all types of education can learn to be effective mediators: coaches, clergy, managers and supervisors, politicians, social workers, principals, crew leaders, parents, police, teachers, board members, therapists, teenagers, small business owners, elders, barbers—anyone who helps settle conflicts in their own corner of the world.

Some types of mediation require more knowledge and skill than most of us learn through life experience alone. Increasingly, professional mediators are expected to have a specialist background and training (labor, divorce, elder/family, employment discrimination, business litigation, education, insurance claims, just to name a few areas).

Even if you don't earn part of your living mediating disputes, there are plenty of conflicts that might benefit from your mediation skills. This book offers several levels of information to suit the needs of every mediator, whether frequent or occasional, official or informal, professional or volunteer.

The anatomy of the mediation process

▶ Similar elements, similar paths

Whether a mediation takes 15 minutes on a playground or involves many parties and dozens of sessions over a period of a year, the process of reaching resolution usually follows a predictable path.

1. First, people present their own views and feelings—often loudly!

2. They share and clarify information, gradually developing a clearer and broader picture of what's going on.

3. If this has eased the emotional strain between them, they move into problem-solving, talking about what they want to change, weighing options, and making decisions.

4. Finally, they write it down, shake hands, or take other action to strengthen their commitment to follow through.

Most mediation processes contain similar elements, because, it seems, this sequence is organic—meaning it *describes* what humans actually do when they resolve conflicts collectively. It will be flavored by culture, personality, and context. It may be messy and reiterative, but these elements seem to be essential for consensual, durable resolutions.

▶ Structure versus "improv"

Context: The process and tools outlined in this handbook are designed for round-the-table mediations where the stakeholders speak directly to each other, and have the authority to reconcile or resolve their dispute without getting permission from others.

Following a structured process can steady both the mediator and the parties, giving a counterweight to the volatile swirl of emotions, accusations, and demands. It slows things down—asking people to take the time to listen, to think, and to learn, *before* they jump to decisions or abandon their efforts at resolution. At the same time, a structured process increases efficiency by focusing people's collective attention, and by laying the foundation for the work of the next phase.

How structured? Mediation is always "improv" to some degree. When people open up, you cannot be sure where it will lead. It's a responsive, adaptive process which gives participants leeway to decide what they want to discuss and how, while offering enough structure that they can have a fresh, productive conversation. If you are new to mediation, we recommend following the process laid out here until it becomes part of your repertoire and you have seen how it works in different settings. Then you will be ready to improvise more freely or restructure.

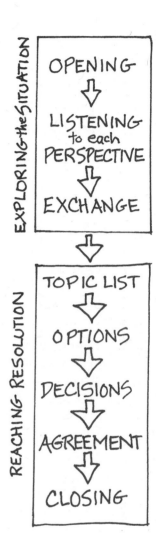

EXPLORING the SITUATION

OPENING ⇩
LISTENING to each PERSPECTIVE ⇩
EXCHANGE

⇩

REACHING RESOLUTION

TOPIC LIST ⇩
OPTIONS ⇩
DECISIONS ⇩
AGREEMENT ⇩
CLOSING

The anatomy of a session

Exploring the situation

1. Opening: Mediators welcome the participants. Then they discuss the proposed purpose and process for the mediation.

2. Listening to each perspective — initial "go-round": Each participant takes a turn speaking, while everyone (including the mediators) listens without questions or comments. People may talk briefly or at length about their view of the situation, and may bring up anything they consider relevant.

3. The Exchange: In open discussion, participants check out misunderstandings and fill in information gaps. They look at specific examples of behaviors and impacts. The focus is on understanding each person's concerns in order to identify their interests and what topics need attention. Often there's de-escalation from a self-protective, adversarial mode towards a readiness to cooperate.

This first half of the mediation digs into the past and the present. It's both an emotional process and a learning process.

Reaching resolution

4. Topic List: The mediator proposes a way to organize the various topics that the participants want to resolve.

5. Options: For each topic in turn, the parties talk through possible options until they come up with something that passes the "gut" test, meets their interests, and is workable.

6. Decisions: Parties review all their decisions, working out the details, and reality-testing to make sure this is workable and what they really want.

7. Agreement: Mediators usually record these decisions in a written agreement.

8. Closing: The parties approve their agreement. The mediators review what has been accomplished, tie up loose ends, and wish them well.

When people are ready, discussion shifts towards the future. How do they want things to be?

Process-centered mediation

Process-centered mediators focus on structuring a conversation and environment that suits the needs, context, and personalities of the participants. The mediator is not only impartial toward the parties, but also neutral toward the outcome—not suggesting, recommending, or favoring particular solutions. Instead, the mediator helps them test whether their ideas meet their interests and are workable and sustainable. Whether or not they reach agreement, if the parties have gotten clearer about the situation, and understand their own needs, options, and best next steps, that is what defines "success."

Participants' goals set the mediator's compass

Our model of mediation is structured around the participants' goals. If the mediators are hoping parties will reconcile a failing partnership but the parties just want a cease-fire and separation, the mediation is in trouble. Likewise, mediators can guide co-workers to negotiate a detailed allotment of tasks, but if the parties are feeling hurt and wanting to mend a friendship, such an agreement can disappoint, and an opportunity for heart-to-heart conversation is missed.

A particular mediation may tilt towards a relationship dialogue on the one hand, or towards a facilitated negotiation on the other, depending on what the parties are seeking:

- Do they hope to repair a relationship?

- Are they looking for a practical solution to a problem?

- Do they need a truce with their adversary that allows them to separate and move on?

- Are they seeking a quicker, less costly substitute for a lawsuit?

- Do they have to make necessary decisions despite tense relations?

And sometimes the only thing they agree on is that it's time to talk.

In our model, it's not the mediator's job to get the parties to reach settlement, to promote empowerment, to solve a problem, or to foster reconciliation, although a mediation may achieve all of these. Instead, the mediator seeks to restore or catalyze the parties' ability to cooperate in meeting each other's reasonable needs and hopes, whatever those may be.

What do you need? How can I help you get there?

1.6
SAMPLE SITUATIONS

➤ Despite her ex-husband Mike's adamant disapproval, Christine has enrolled their oldest in a private religious elementary school, and is demanding Mike pay the tuition, as he has done for preschool and kindergarten. The two cannot stand being in the same room with each other, but to avoid a costly court battle, they are trying mediation.

➤ Gene and Chris are students who share an apartment. That went fine until Gene got a new girlfriend, who is around most of the time. Gene contacted campus mediation because Chris owes him two months of rent and utilities. He needs the cash now! But Chris says not until the girlfriend pays her third.

Guiding principles

The guiding principles below are the reasons WHY we, the authors, choose to do this work, and serve as guidelines for HOW we mediate.

Respect

➤ Value each person's experience, concerns, needs, and dignity.

➤ Assume that each person is capable of acting cooperatively with goodwill and integrity.

It's not always easy to stay respectful when you are dealing with people who are on the attack or in victim mode, who may be lying, or who have made what seem to you to be stupid or destructive decisions.

It's their life: Self-determination

The parties are the "experts" about their situation. In mediation, they speak for themselves, think for themselves, and decide for themselves. The mediator supports people in doing this with greater clarity and thoughtfulness, but it is the participants who do the hard work of figuring out how to resolve their concerns.

Mediation helps organizations and communities to resolve problems close to the source. The people directly involved plan their futures, not needing to rely on external authorities to decide and enforce.

Dialogue: Listening and talking it out

The goal is to get the parties listening to each other, talking with each other face-to-face (rather than using the mediator as a go-between, or talking through their lawyers).

Cooperative alternatives to coercion

We seek to help build a society and culture that practices active, non-coercive ways of resolving conflicts and strengthening relationships. Mediation gives parties a way to meet their needs without fighting or caving in. It offers accessible, low-tech collaborative tools for a world that often seems overwhelmed with conflicts over resources, identity, and self-determination. In the face of our human capacity to damage ourselves and our environment in the blink of an eye, developing sophisticated approaches to cooperation is not just "nice," it is critical if we human beings are to survive on this planet.

**1.7
SAMPLE SITUATIONS**

➤ CrossCurrent Hospital has had trouble getting patients to pay their bills. They institute a mediation option, and mediators are eventually able to help them design a new set of payment options that are more feasible for their customers, thus resulting in fewer disputes.

➤ A woman charges a bunch of young teens in her neighborhood with harassment. The judge calls a mediator team to facilitate a meeting in the court building. In the first go-round, each boy speaks. "We were just having some fun." The woman then talks about her diabetes, her troubled children, the loss of her job. When she talks of the disrespect the boys showed her, she sobs. No agreement is necessary; each boy apologizes. The fun has gone out of it.

Mediation terms

CONCERN	INTERPRETATION	POSITION	INTEREST	TOPIC
Their problems and complaints. What they want changed, fixed, or to be compensated for.	Meanings they give to the information they have: Explanations, perceived motives, generalizations, judgments, mind-reads, worries.	Their public stance about what should happen, what is right: demands, requests, principles, threats.	What really matters to this person, what motivates them. What future they want.	A subject the parties need to discuss and decide—stated so as to include all parties.
Barking dog.	Neighbor is unfriendly, inconsiderate. Violates my privacy.	Buy a muzzle. Keep the dog indoors.	I'm not well. I need my sleep. To have my home be a quiet, private place.	Dog's barking at night.
Unfair bill.	This company wants to rip me off! They think I'm not smart enough to notice.	I will not pay for work you didn't even do.	To be treated fairly. To know what something will cost so I can budget for it.	What work was done, what recompense, if any, is fair. How rest of job will be billed.
Rude treatment, exclusion from meetings.	This guy is a snake. He's undermining me in front of my boss.	You owe me an apology.	To keep my good reputation. Less stress at work.	Who attends meetings. How people speak to each other.
Tenant owes me 3 months back rent.	Tenant is a freeloader. Tenant may go bankrupt.	Pay $1,600 this week or I'll evict you!	Fairness. To get the money, have reliable income.	Payment plan. Repair plan.

This table will give you a feel for how we use these main mediation terms. We chose the broader, more sympathetic term "concern" in place of "complaint" or "problem;" likewise, the neutral "participant" for individuals and "party" for one or more participants who are on the "same side." Because "issue" is a loose word with various meanings, we use the more precise word "topic."

GETTING TO THE TABLE

THE PROCESS

2

Can mediation help this situation?

 ## Yes, it's worth a try

Mediation works in a surprisingly wide variety of conflicts and contexts. The type of dispute is less predictive of success than whether *you* can picture a mediation working out, and whether, in your judgment, the following apply:

PEOPLE	• They are capable of participating—some ability and willingness to express themselves, to converse, to make decisions. • They want resolution: At least some of those involved need and honestly want a resolution. Good intentions do not guarantee good outcomes, but they help.
CONTENT	• Positive action is possible. The source of the dispute—what the fight is about—can potentially change if people's behavior changes.

▶ No, probably not

Even when the above conditions are present, you may still advise another pathway. Maybe another forum will give them better results, or mediation needs to happen in tandem with other efforts, such as coaching, therapy, organizational restructuring, or community development.

Additionally, if any of the following apply, be wary of recommending mediation:

PEOPLE	• A participant is not able to grasp the complexities of the issues or their legal options. • There have been threats of violence. There's a history of pathological, addictive, or abusive behavior.
CONTENT	• Investigation and disclosure is necessary before a fair negotiation can take place. • A participant feels the dispute deserves public attention rather than a private resolution (e.g., to prevent more victimization, to establish precedent, to influence policies).
DECISIONS	• There's a wide gap in power, and the weaker party is not prepared or can't afford counsel. • Parties see mediation as a tool for retaliation or for bolstering their court case. • Decision-makers are not present. • People who may be affected by a decision or whose cooperation is necessary are not represented.

How people find a mediator

2.1
INFORMAL WAYS TO DESCRIBE MEDIATION

- *If it's helpful, I could be present when you and the owners talk this over.*

- *Would you like me to be there when you meet with her?*

- *Having a third person there might help keep the conversation on track.*

- *Let's get together and see what you all can work out.*

▶ Direct contact

➤ **Seeking a mediator.** Parties usually turn to a mutually trusted person to facilitate a difficult conversation. If they want privacy or high skill, they may seek out a professional mediator from the growing number of private-sector, non-profit, and government mediation services.

➤ **Approaching disputing parties.** If you want to offer your services for a dispute that seems ripe for mediation, approach it strategically: Who is the best person to raise this possibility with each party? How can you reassure them that you are competent and not secretly an advocate for one party?

➤ **You may want to offer a no-obligation consult to each party**, so they can judge whether mediation (and you) are right for them.

➤ **You don't have to call it a mediation.** Often the notion of "mediating" their dispute embarrasses people, or feels uncomfortably formal. You can describe it in everyday language instead, or use terms that de-emphasize "conflict" — for example, a meeting, a clearing-the-air session, a team-building day, or a planning session.

▶ Referrals

Many mediations come through referral sources.

➤ **Through institutions**, typically courts, school personnel, human-resources departments, and social-service agencies. In most places, mediators are called in as needed. In high-conflict environments, mediators may be present just in case, say in a courthouse or on a playground.

➤ **Lawyer-initiated.** The parties' lawyers may decide that a case is now ready for a mediated settlement. They may select the mediators, too.

➤ **Required by contract.** Some contracts provide for mediation before resorting to arbitration or litigation. Usually parties select professional mediators from a predetermined list or set of criteria.

➤ **Standard practice in an industry or within an organization.** Mediation has long been an option in labor-management disputes, and in some industries people now routinely mediate commercial, customer, and employment disputes. Some large organizations have their own internal "ombuds" office or mediation program.

Voluntary or mandatory?

▶ Voluntary versus mandatory participation

People sometimes find themselves in mediation because a manager, a judge, or an agency sent them there. So-called "mandatory mediation" means required attendance, not "mandatory agreement," though not reaching one may result in negative consequences for the parties.

Mandatory attendance raises ethical questions about safety, about reluctant agreements, and about pressure to reveal information and feelings. On the practical side, it can inhibit participants' willingness to participate in good faith, to be forthright, to show vulnerability, or to come up with unorthodox solutions.

Can mediation still be a respectful, egalitarian, and self-determined process under these circumstances? The hard truth is that many people would never even try mediation without *some* kind of pressure (if not from an institution, it may come from a friend, a relative, or the other party). Mediators need to decide where to draw the line in their own practice.

If you accept a "mandatory" mediation case, let the participants know what latitude they have. Can they choose to leave the mediation at any time? What will the referral source be told about the discussion or about the agreement? What will they be told if the participants don't reach agreement? Fortunately, even in mandated mediations, once parties get into discussion they can be surprised to find themselves—really—resolving their conflict after all.

▶ Working with the referral source

Use the sidebar checklist when a case is referred to you. If you get many referrals from one source, work with the institution on what kinds of cases are suitable for mediation. Review how they screen and educate the parties so they arrive prepared and willing. What information do you need from the source up front? What materials do they want you to provide? What can they expect from you afterwards?

Look for opportunities to appreciate the people who refer situations to you, remembering to maintain impartiality and confidentiality.

2.2
REFERRAL CHECKLIST

✓ Why do they think the parties could benefit from mediation?

✓ What have they told the parties about mediation?

✓ Are they suggesting, persuading, pressuring, or requiring the parties to go?

✓ What interventions has the referral source tried already? Any other useful background information?

✓ Your policies on reporting back, on confidentiality, on voluntary participation. Fees, if relevant.

✓ Are there procedures or charges pending? Do participants need to contact them again after the mediation if they reach agreement—or if they don't?

Initial conversations

SUMMARY:
INITIAL CONVERSATION

Step One: Do they want to participate?

- **Listen and reflect back.**

- **Describe mediation.**

- **Discuss their concerns about mediation.**

Step Two: Preparing for the mediation

- **Define the scope of the mediation**

- **Approach the other parties**

- **Logistics**

▶ Purpose: Decide whether to mediate

Getting people who are embroiled in a hot dispute to sit down at a table together can be more challenging than the mediation itself. During this pre-mediation phase, the mediator has one-on-one conversations with those involved to help them decide whether to participate, find out who needs to attend, and explore how the mediation should be structured. You are also auditioning for the mediator role! Helping them reach an agreement to mediate will take just as much attention, empathy, and skill as mediating the session will.

You may set up a session after a single conversation with each party, or it may take some back and forth. Avoid surprises! If possible, speak with *each* participant in advance, so they and you are fully prepared. Even people on the same "side" of a conflict may have very different perspectives, goals, and level of interest in participating.

Step One: Do they want to participate? You listen and reflect back, explain the process, time commitment, and cost—and address their questions and concerns. They consider whether they want to mediate. Meanwhile, you assess whether mediation is appropriate.

Step Two: Preparing for the mediation. Who else do they think needs to participate in order to resolve the situation? Explore how to approach those others about the idea. Set a goal for the process that all parties can align with. Once everyone's agreed, focus on the logistics of setting up the sessions.

Do they want to participate?

Put on your impartial and attentive mediation hat from the very beginning: Think of the mediation as starting the first moment you speak with one of the parties.

▶ Listen first

It's no use trying to persuade someone to mediate until they feel listened to, and have a chance to test your understanding and skill. It can sometimes take a full hour to hear their concerns, to show how you respond, and to explain how mediation might help.

➤ **Invite them to talk about the situation** and reassure them that it's confidential. Listen and reflect back their concerns. [**See pages 101, 128.**]

➤ **Ask for examples** to understand the specific behaviors that concern them, and the practical and emotional impact it's had on them.

➤ **They are testing you, not just the idea of mediation.** Show in your responses that you take their feelings and concerns seriously—that you "get it."

➤ Show empathy without treating their concerns as facts.

> *So from your point of view, he was bullying you?* (Not: "So he was bullying you?")

> *So you got a sense that he disliked your work?* (Not: "So he disliked your work?")

▶ Describe how mediation might work

Describe how a mediation might look in *their particular situation*, how it could help them get what they want and need, rather than talking about mediation in general:

> *You'll be able to talk about the impact of being laid off, he'll have a chance to respond, then I'll help you both talk it over. If he starts yelling like you described, I will stop him.*

> *We'll figure out what topics to cover—such as dividing property, financial support, parenting decisions and parenting schedule. Sounds like you'll also want to discuss how to pay for Dan's college.*

> *I would help you come up with ideas. We could explore the option you said she wouldn't listen to, about splitting the debt 60/40—and other ideas.*

> *You'd be able to come up with solutions that work for you instead of having a judge decide what will happen.*

About the conflict

- *What's been happening?*

- *What matters most?*

- *What's at stake for you? For your company?*

- *What makes you want to resolve this?*

- *What keeps you from giving up?*

About whether they want to mediate

- *How have you tried to resolve this already? How well has it worked?*

- *What do you hope to get out of a mediation?*

- *What hesitations do you have?*

- *What are you afraid might happen if you come to mediation?*

- *What might happen if you don't mediate?*

- *What are your other options?*

Do they want to participate?

▶ Discuss their concerns about mediation

➤ **Acknowledge their concerns** about trying mediation. Discuss how you might structure mediation in a way that meets those concerns.

➤ **Explain that everyone feels apprehensive beforehand** because it's a hard thing to do, and an unfamiliar setting, but that the process is well-designed to make it easier to work things through.

➤ **If they are nervous about meeting face to face** with the other party, discuss what they fear might happen. Help them think about positive ways they might respond, and how you might be able to support them.

➤ **Caution: only promise what YOU can do as mediator.** You can't guarantee how other participants will behave or what the outcome of a session might be.

Help them assess other options

➤ **Have they tried talking directly to the other person?** If not, explore whether it would make sense to do that first, and how they might approach it. You might offer to be a behind-the-scenes coach rather than a mediator.

➤ **Have they considered other ways this might be resolved besides mediation?** You might suggest they consult other third-party resources (arbitrator, lawyer, police, counselor, pastor) or explore other approaches (filing a grievance, using social services, consulting their manager).

➤ **Do they need time to think it over?** Confronting someone face to face can be a risk. If they decide to try mediation but still sound uneasy, you may want to suggest they sleep on it and call you tomorrow.

▶ Screening

For some types of disputes, you may need to screen for situations or personalities that should only be mediated by people with other kinds of relevant professional expertise, if at all.

Keep an ear out for indications of abuse, addiction, delusion, undue subservience or pressure to participate, the presence of weapons or other dangerous threats. Word your questions carefully to encourage truthful answers.

Defining the scope

▶ Help them describe the scope they want

➤ What type of outcome would make mediation worthwhile? (Draw this more broadly than their specific demands and positions.) Who would need to take part?

> *If you and the other partners can't agree on a new business plan, you'd like to agree how to dissolve the partnership as fairly and inexpensively as possible?*

➤ **Define a scope that's realistic** given who's willing to participate, what decisions they can make, how much time and resources they have:

> *You want Josie to feel you've considered her input and still recognize that, as her supervisor you have the authority to assign and oversee her work.*

➤ **Help them have realistic expectations.** Focus on outcomes they can accomplish without relying on others to cooperate or approve. If you think their hopes are unrealistic, ask some "what if" questions. [**See page 165.**]

> *It sounds like you want to keep the conversation business-like and finish in one session. Sometimes people have to talk about how an accident affected them before they are ready to accept a cash settlement. What if that's the case with Walter?*

Define the mediation's scope in mutually agreeable terms

As you speak with everyone who will participate, look to define a scope that you think everyone can align with, and that leaves open options about how you might guide the sessions to get there:

> *From speaking with all of you, it sounds like you'd all like to explore how to reduce tensions among GoodWorks board members and the CEO. Does that describe what you want mediation to do?*

> *It's clear you all love this land and want to stay. Everyone's willing to participate in a process to come up with a plan for sustainable development, even if it takes several months.*

2.4
QUESTIONS TO DECIDE MEDIATION SCOPE

- *What concerns do you hope mediation will resolve?*

- *What's your overall goal for the outcome of the mediation?*

- *Who needs to participate in order to meet that goal?*

- *If just the two of you meet and come up with new ideas, will you need someone else's input and assent?*

- *How will you know when the mediation work is done?*

- *How much time do you have to make this decision?*

Approaching the other parties

▶ Approaching the other parties

Non-initiating parties may reject an invitation to mediate without giving it much thought. They may assume that the mediator is aligned with the initiating party. Or they may simply think that anything the other party requests has got to be a bad idea.

These parties may need a personal reference before they even consider mediation as an option. If possible, you want that assurance to come from someone they know and trust.

Consider using an intermediary if the person you're talking with is uneasy about inviting the other parties directly, and thinks they might also dismiss a call from you. This usually involves having the first party ask "Jack"—a mutual friend who has the trust of the other party—to interview you. If Jack agrees that mediation might be useful, ask if he would broach the idea with the other party:

> *I've found it works best if you or someone else asks the other party to call me, instead of me calling them directly.*

> *If I contact the other party by phone or email, do you think they'd be open to the idea? If you ask them to call me, do you think they probably will?*

> *Is there someone the other party trusts, who might be willing to call me if you asked? They could interview me and decide if they want to suggest that the other party contact me.*

2.5
WHO SHOULD ATTEND

With each person you talk to, ask:

- *Your concerns about work distribution and scheduling are management decisions. Should your manager attend?*

- *Who needs to participate in order to meet that goal?*

- *If just the two of you meet and come up with new ideas, will you need your mother's input and assent?*

- *You want to discuss with your brothers what to do with the beach house. What role will your spouses have in that decision?*

Approaching the other parties

▶ Talking with the other parties

Your pre-mediation conversation with the other parties follows the same guidelines as before, with some additional considerations:

➤ **Explain your purpose:**

> *Benjamin contacted me about having a mediated conversation, and when I asked who needed to be part of it, he suggested that I get in touch with you.*

> *I'm offering each person a free consultation, so you can talk with me and decide for yourself whether I might be helpful.*

➤ **Explain your impartial role and assure confidentiality:**

> *All my conversations are confidential, including this one.*

➤ **Don't tell, ask.** They may want to know what the other party has said to you. Don't tell them. Simply explain your practice and focus on their options:

> *I can't speak for them directly, but I know they are interested in having a discussion to figure out how to make this better.*

➤ **Neutral language.** Take care not to describe the situation using words and viewpoints you've picked up from other participants you've talked to already!

➤ **Show that you empathize with their concerns** and are not representing or favoring the other party.

➤ **Be prepared for a "no problem" response.** If they claim to have no problem with the other party, explore what might happen if they don't respond to the other party's concerns.

▶ Getting to know the parties

As you talk to each party, notice:

➤ How are you reacting to this person?

➤ How do they present themselves?

➤ What communication patterns do you notice?

➤ Is their perspective narrow or broad, rigid or open?

This can help you to understand why they have become stuck in this conflict, and what mediation approaches you might try.

Should I be the mediator?

**2.6
SHOULD I BE THE
MEDIATOR?**

✓ Do I feel comfortable
and competent when
talking with these
people about their
situation?

✓ Can I be impartial?
Do I have a stake in
the solution?

✓ Will I be seen as
impartial? How does
getting paid vs.
volunteering affect
this?

✓ If the mediation does
not go well, might
there be negative
fallout for me?

✓ Can they politely
say no?

▶ Expertise and respect

Solid mediation skills are sufficient for many disputes. However, you must have a baseline familiarity with the parties' context, and you must have the parties' respect. In some cases, you will be required or well-advised to have specialized training to mediate conflicts for example where family-systems, legal, financial, or other technical knowledge is needed.

➤ **Baseline knowledge.** Are you up to speed on the concepts, vocabulary, issues, and types of agreements common in this kind of dispute? Do you understand the politics, the environment, and the social norms well enough to do reality testing?

➤ **The parties' respect.** Do the parties think you are at their level? They may care more about the mediator's personal and professional credentials than about the person's mediation skill.

▶ If you have a connection to the parties

Can you be fair and impartial? Equally important, will the other participants SEE you as fair and impartial?

Be up front with everyone about any connection you have with any participant. Check privately whether anyone feels constrained by this fact. Make it easy for them to say no to you as mediator if they are not comfortable for any reason. (Maybe have someone else ask.)

▶ Working with a co-mediator

We strongly recommend mediating with a partner at least some of the time, as it brings a host of benefits:

➤ **Sharing the work** increases the mediators' collective knowledge and skill. A partner can help you think, be a second pair of ears and eyes, back you up or take the lead, scribe on the board, or talk to one party while you talk to the other.

➤ **A team can better reflect participants' various identities** and backgrounds.

➤ **Watching other mediators work** and getting feedback can improve and expand your own skills, whatever your level of experience.

Note: Mediate a routine situation together before taking on a major case, if you can. For suggestions about how to prepare for a mediation together, see page 29.

Pre-mediation agreements and review

Double-check this list as you prepare for the mediation sessions. You can go over these points at the beginning of the session, or write them in a "Mediation Participation Agreement."

Roles

✓ Confirm everyone's understanding of the mediation's scope, their shared goal for mediation, and their roles as participants.

✓ Review your role as mediator, including what you mean by "impartial" and "neutral." You will facilitate the sessions, in consultation with them. You will not recommend or evaluate solutions or fault, or give legal advice. Encourage them to seek expert advice if you or they think it advisable.

✓ Disclose any connections you have with the subject matter or parties.

✓ List who will be there, including lawyers, support people, and their role (participant, observer). Be clear that no one else may attend without X days' notice, your prior approval, and all parties' consent.

✓ Check that their expectations of you and of themselves are realistic—what can be accomplished, what you can do for them.

Conditions

✓ Information each side promises to disclose, such as finances.

✓ Confidentiality—who can communicate what to whom outside the room; policy on recording or taking photos.

✓ What topics will or won't be discussed at the table.

✓ How and when they—and you—can withdraw from the process.

✓ Commitment not to subpoena you or mediation documents in any lawsuit.

✓ Liability releases that protect you as mediator.

Logistics

✓ **Place, accessibility:** Ask each person about accessibility needs, including transportation, and confirm all location arrangements you make. [**See page 107.**]

✓ **Dates & times:** Schedule two sessions up front, and agree on firm start and end times.

✓ **Fees**, payment arrangements.

✓ **Forms** that are specific to your mediation practice.

Choosing a location

▶ What location works best?

Discuss with participants what place would be convenient, comfortable, and accessible, and feel neutral to them. It doesn't have to be a meeting room — you may find that a picnic bench, a walk on the beach, or an expensive restaurant creates the right atmosphere. Some considerations:

➤ **A place that doesn't "belong" to one party.** Shared territory is okay, off-site is usually better, even if it's just a café down the street.

➤ **Away from it all.** An off-site location may encourage a fresh start. Being "away" can reduce other distractions and interruptions, and offer privacy if confidentiality is important. On the other hand, unfamiliar spaces may increase the participants' unease — and cost more.

➤ **The mediator's turf.** Even if your home or office is pleasant, and most convenient for you, make sure it is the right atmosphere for them.

➤ **Comfortable environment.** The space should fit with cultural norms, the closeness of the relationship, the formality of the parties, and accessibility needs.

▶ What makes a good space?

There are few perfect spaces and many considerations:

✓ **Privacy.** Find a place where you will not be overheard or distracted.

✓ **Schedule.** Ensure that you will not be interrupted or have to leave before you are ready.

✓ **Pleasant atmosphere.** The facility should offer the level of formality and amenities your participants expect. Fresh air and pleasant lighting help. Even if participants are only subliminally aware of pleasant surroundings, it signals respect and reduces stress.

✓ **Right-sized.** A large room can feel "cold"; a small one can make some people feel that the other participants are intimidatingly close.

✓ **Secondary space** for private Separate Conversations.

✓ **Seating.** Identical chairs, comfortable for several hours of sitting, are best.

✓ **Table,** if you want to use one. Will everyone fit? Is it small enough that everyone can hear and see and feel like part of a group, but large enough that they aren't uncomfortably close?

THE MEDIATION SESSION PART I: EXPLORING THE SITUATION

EXPLORING the SITUATION

OPENING
⇩
LISTENING
to each
PERSPECTIVE
⇩
EXCHANGE

THE PROCESS

3

Preparing yourself, co-mediators

The next two chapters lay out the steps of a mediation session, from the time the mediators walk in the door, through wrapping up. Real life may not be so linear, but if you're new to mediation, follow this sequence as closely as you can.

▶ Prepare yourself

✓ Minimize your own stresses, so that you are free to concentrate for the full session, not dashing in or dashing away or waiting for a vital phone call. Try to be rested, to have eaten well.

✓ Review notes and information (though some mediators prefer to go in with a "blank-slate" mind). Plan how you'd like to open.

✓ Give yourself plenty of time to set up and shift your attention to the mediation. Be forewarned that parties sometimes arrive quite early!

✓ If interpreters or other support people will be helping with the mediation, talk with them in advance about how you would like to work with them.

▶ Confer with your co-mediators

If you are working as a pair or a team, prepare enough that you can genuinely and easily use "we." In addition to going over the particulars of the upcoming mediation, you'll probably want to discuss working together:

Divide up tasks

✓ **Preparation:** Talking with referral sources, pre-session work with the parties, managing fees and paperwork, setting up the space.

✓ **Session:** The Opening bullet points, timekeeping, recording on the board or chart, writing up the agreement.

Coordinate your facilitation

✓ Your facilitation styles, pace, models, and philosophy.

✓ Who will take the lead when, how to signal or pass the ball.

✓ When is it okay to consult with each other openly at the table, when do you prefer a private conversation?

✓ Anything you'd like the other mediator to observe or help with, in terms of improving your own skills.

Setting up

▶ Arranging the room

The room is the stage of the mediation theater. You want to create a pleasant atmosphere that helps everyone settle into a serious and cooperative session. We can't stress enough the difference surroundings can make. [**See page 26.**]

✓ **If you aren't familiar with the place**, arrive extra early—it can take a while to make a space comfortable. If a facilities person is on duty, check in with them. Locate the building's entrances, elevators, and bathrooms.

✓ **Set up the furniture and flip chart** if you're using one. In large rooms, make a cozier space at one end of it. Prepare a waiting area for Separate Conversations. Clear away extra chairs and clutter.

✓ **Organize your materials**—packets for participants, your own notes, etc. Test your markers, the printer connection. Remember that anything lying out on the table may be read by wandering eyes!

✓ **Put out water**, and consider also providing drinks and snacks.

One way to ease initial tensions is to delay finishing the setup and enlist participants to help you move furniture, fill water pitchers, etc. This tip from mentor Charlie Walker has worked like a charm many times.

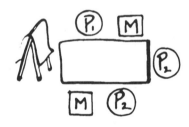

▶ Seating

Often there's no need to assign seats, but whatever you decide, make sure:

✓ Everyone can see everyone else and the board or flip chart.

✓ Members of one party can sit together.

✓ The seating suggests mediator impartiality.

✓ There's a table between them if they have a history of intimidation or fights.

Think about what kind of mood the seating pattern might create. Do you want a friendly "living room" circle of comfortable chairs or a business-like conference table? Are the mediators presiding at the head of the table or sitting around it with the participants? Should the participants be directly opposite each other or at a softer angle?

Opening

▶ Purpose

The Opening creates the "framework" for the mediation, setting a tone and building shared expectations. It's the time to:

➤ **Let parties get used to sitting in the same room** with people they may dislike or fear.

➤ **Give mediators a feel for the participants,** their mood, their self-awareness, and their communication patterns.

➤ **Address the parties' unspoken questions:**

- "Will the mediator really listen to me?"

- "Is this mediator capable of dealing with these (other) people?"

- "What is going to happen, and how am I supposed to participate?"

- "Will I be forced to give in?"

- "What good is this? This mediator has no power to make those people behave! And she looks clueless…"

There's a lot of information to cover during the Opening; however, this is secondary to creating a connection—to you, to the process, to their hopes. Participants are more likely to tune in when a mediator talks *with* them, not *at* them, and adapts the level of detail to what they can take in.

Opening: Welcome & warm-up

3.1
WARM-UP QUESTIONS

Ask about them:

Before we get started here, could you tell us a bit about…?

- *Your children… (custody dispute).*

- *Your role in the organization.*

- *One thing you like about your neigh-borhood.*

Ask about mediation:

We don't want to get into details yet, but could you tell us briefly…

- *What made you decide to come today?*

- *What's your hope for what will happen today?*

- *Even though the judge required that you give this a try, what could happen today that would make it worth your time?*

▶ Greeting the parties

➤ **Greet each person by name.**

➤ **Make small talk with care.** To avoid suspicions of bias, refrain from lively chatting with the first arrival and keep somewhat of a physical distance. Set them at ease, but don't discuss the dispute or the other parties. Draw in new arrivals right away—*We were just talking about…* and move to get started with the session.

➤ **If one party doesn't show up**, don't discuss substantive issues with the people who *did* come if there's any chance you might mediate this situation later.

▶ Welcome & warm-up

Once everyone is seated and settled in:

➤ **Confirm names again,** including repeating the mediators' names.

➤ **Thank them for being willing to come.** Reassure them that although mediation may not be easy, in your experience it can often make difficult situations much better.

Warm up with a brief conversation

A soft entry may help break the ice. [**See sidebar.**] Here are some starting points:

➤ Ask a positive question, something easy to answer about a positive aspect of their life that avoids areas of contention.

➤ Or ask a diagnostic question about expectations, goals, or their feelings about trying this mediation.

Make clear that you are looking for just a few sentences, and make sure you get responses from each person. This signals from the outset that the mediation is about them, about their voices. It also gives you a few minutes to get a sense of the participants.

➤ If they start to slip into discussing conflict content, ask them to hold off for a few minutes until you've explained how the mediation will work.

➤ If they say they were forced to come and don't want to be present, let them know that, in fact, participation is voluntary, but that you hope they'll give it a try since they're here already. [**See page 17.**]

Opening: Participants' role, willingness

The participants' role

✓ **Each participant decides what's important**, what their priorities are. You will not tell them what to decide or press them to sign anything they don't fully agree to.

✓ **Speaking, listening, thinking:** You hope they will feel comfortable and safe enough to:

- Speak openly about their concerns and share information.
- Listen for what's new and important.
- Note ideas that could make the situation better for everyone.

✓ **Supporters:** Review when and how attorneys, interpreters, and other supporters may take part.

✓ **Share required information**, e.g., in divorce mediation, you require disclosure of all finances.

Participant confidentiality

✓ **Check about confidentiality:** Do they prefer to have a confidential conversation today? Note that, as mediator, you can't guarantee what participants will say or do afterward. If they have concerns, help them work it out either now or before the go-round.

✓ **No recording or photos**, neither by the parties nor the mediators, not even of board/chart notes, which can be taken out of context.

The flow of the mediation session

✓ **Sketch out the process.** [See sidebar.]

✓ **Breaks & consultations:** Anyone is welcome to ask for a break, or for time to confer privately.

✓ **Separate Conversations:** At some stage, you may meet with each party alone. Say this up front, so they aren't taken by surprise later.

Willingness to go ahead

✓ **Ask if they have any questions about the process.** (This seems to work better than asking whether they have worries or hesitations.)

✓ **Be open to adjusting your process** if you think their ideas will work and you're comfortable doing it.

✓ **Ask, *Are you willing to give this a try?*** Get clear assent from everyone.

3.4
QUICK SESSION OVERVIEW

To start, each of you will have a turn to speak about what has been happening and how it has affected you. Next we'll explore your concerns in detail, the impact it's had, filling in information gaps, finding out what each of you most wants and needs.

In the second part of the session, we'll focus on the future—the topics you need to resolve or decide.

We will take the time for you to find resolutions that truly meet your needs, and will be workable. We'll record the decisions you make in a written agreement.

It's a lot for 2½ hours, but I think you can do it! If not, we have another session on the calendar two weeks from now.

Listening to Each Perspective

SUMMARY: LISTENING TO EACH PERSPECTIVE

1. **Explain how a "go-round" works**

2. **Ask an open-ended starting question**

3. **Steer minimally if at all**

4. **Protect each person's speaking time**

5. **Check, thank, move on to the next person**

▶ Purpose: A chance to speak and to listen

The Listening to Each Perspective go-round gives each participant a chance to relate their experience, describe their concerns, make their claims, and express their feelings—without interruption or challenge. It also gives mediators a feel for the speaker's state of mind, how they think, and where the distress is. (If there are just two participants, you explain it as "each having a turn" instead of a "go-round.")

▶ Explain how the go-round works

1. *Each of you will have a turn to speak about the situation.*

2. *Save any responses, comments, or questions for later. Note down anything you want to remember to say.*

3. *Try to notice anything the speaker says that's new to you.*

➤ **Every participant gets a turn**, including those in the same party—but not the observers, if any. If lawyers are present, and by agreement are making opening statements, still give each client a chance to speak as well.

➤ **Act as if everyone will respect the go-round.** Most will. You and the participants can establish guidelines later if they are having difficulty.

➤ **No need to set a time limit** unless you have more than about four participants. Some will have more to say, or take longer to say it.

Listening to Each Perspective

▶ Ask an open-ended starting question

➤ **Ask who would be willing to go first.** Don't make a big deal of it, parties rarely quarrel about this. If you have some reason for asking one party to start, don't explain your choice, just say, *Alex, why don't you start?*

➤ **Suggest the others listen for anything new**, anything they didn't already know. Remind them to jot down a note rather than respond.

➤ **Ask your opening question in a tone that shows you care** about hearing their answer.

▶ Steer minimally

When mediators listen quietly, it helps create a receptive mood and respects how each person chooses to relate their experience.

➤ **Save your questions for later**, unless you don't understand what they're saying, or they've been overly brief or vague.

➤ **Resist the impulse to reflect back or summarize.** You will do a lot of that later, but for now let their own words stand, without implying that you are judging, improving, or translating what they have to say.

When the speaker gets off track

There are some situations where the mediator does say something:

➤ **You need information to follow their account.** (*Who is Richard?*)

➤ **Repeating.** Step in to summarize and ask if they have covered the main things they wanted to bring up. Then inquire, *Would it make sense for Tina to take a turn now?*

➤ **Endless details.** Some people expect to tell their story ALL the way from the beginning. They may not know how to outline their main points, or to leave out some details — even when asked to. Consider using a series of shorter go-rounds, each with a more limited question: *What happened last week? What upsets you most?*

➤ **Not saying much.** Give a few prompts — *Is there anything else you want to mention now? Could you say a bit about what the impact has been?* Don't press — there will be time to find out more during the Exchange.

**3.6
OPEN-ENDED
STARTING QUESTIONS**

(Pick just ONE!)

- *Will you tell us about the situation from your point of view?*

- *What's been happening, and how does it affect you?*

- *What's the history of this situation, and what have you tried so far to resolve it?*

- *What concerns would you like to make sure we talk about today?*

If antagonism seems high, try a more focused question:

- *What topics do we need to talk about here today in order to resolve the situation?*

- *Would you summarize what's most important to you?*

Listening to Each Perspective

3.7
WHEN THEY INTERRUPT

• I know it's hard to listen... There will be plenty of time to respond and discuss after we finish the go-round.

• Let's let Tina finish her turn. Would it help to jot yourself a note to bring it up later?

• I still need to hear how Tina experienced it. Then we'll dive into those parts where your perspectives differ.

Frank: ...then you smashed my car windows. Didn't you!

Eric, bursting in: How dare you accuse me? It was you who...

Mediator: *Frank, can you explain the situation to me instead of to Eric? It is hard for people not to answer back when you speak to them directly. So you found your car window smashed...?*

⬛ Protect each person's speaking time

When people are having trouble listening

➤ **Quietly ask them to hold back** during the other person's turn, and to write themselves a note. Use a warm, respectful tone.

➤ **Acknowledge that it can be hard to listen.**

➤ **Suggest that the speaker tell YOU instead** of talking directly to the other party. (It's nearly impossible for listeners not to respond to finger-pointing accusations or direct questions, e.g., "Why did you slash our tires?") Aim to get them back to talking to each other once the go-round ends.

➤ **Cope.** If one participant seems incapable of staying quiet, don't stress about it. Keep your attention on the current speaker.

➤ **Move into the Exchange.** If all parties are eagerly engaged in useful discussion, go with their momentum. When there's a lull in the conversation, you can say, *Before we continue, not everyone got a full turn back there. Does anyone want to bring up something that hasn't been mentioned yet?*

⬛ Check, thank, move to the next person

➤ **Check:** *Is there anything else you want to bring up at this point?*

➤ **Thank them.**

➤ **Repeat your opening question for the next person.** If they start by responding specifically to something that's been said, you may want to stop them gently and encourage them to start off by explaining their view of the situation, rather than by responding.

➤ **Offering people a chance for a second go-round** may sometimes be useful — for example, if the first speaker said much less than the people who followed.

The Exchange

SUMMARY: THE EXCHANGE

1. Invite questions and responses

2. Clear up misinformation, gaps

3. Explore concerns: examples of behavior + impact

4. Summarize interests

Throughout:

- **Encourage empathy, reconciliation**

- **Postpone discussing solutions!**

▶ Purpose: Finding out what matters

After each person has presented their perspective, they begin open discussion, a phase we call the Exchange. This face-to-face conversation about people's concerns and hopes is the heart of the mediation.

Our mediation colleague Chel Avery explains it this way: "The Exchange is like cleaning out your closet… It looks like a huge unpleasant mess, and you wonder how you'll ever organize it. But first you have to start by dumping all the stuff out and seeing what is there."

As the sketch on page 41 shows, the Exchange starts out with a jumble of accounts, claims, demands, interpretations, concerns. The mediator helps participants sort through it, gradually building a clearer, shared picture of their situation. Ideally a shift happens on two fronts:

- From a self-centered view ➡ to a situation-centered view.

- From adversarial mode ➡ to cooperative mode.

By the end, people should have more accurate information, have identified what interests need to be met in order to resolve their conflict, and be ready for problem-solving. In some cases, they may also have experienced emotional relief and more empathy for the other side.

The Exchange: Facilitating

Lots of things are going on during the Exchange! Before we look at the particular tasks, here are some overall facilitation tips:

Support the people

➤ **Listen carefully.**

➤ Be patient, unhurried, accepting.

➤ Work WITH the way they are participating. You are unlikely to change people's behavior or attitudes.

➤ Focus on what their emotions reveal about the situation rather than on the emotion itself. For example, ask, *What disappointed you?* not "How did that make you feel?"

➤ Prevent hostile exchanges.

➤ Don't try to persuade them of *anything*.

Manage the process

➤ Get them talking to each other rather than to you.

➤ Use visuals such as a flip chart to organize the discussion.

➤ Consult them about process decisions.

➤ Use acknowledging [**see page 101**] and other rewording tools [**see pages 128–131**]: reflect back, prompt, summarize content, orient them to where they are in the process, ask "what & how" questions, reframe.

Gather information for problem-solving

➤ Use their goals for the process as your compass.

➤ Draw out substantive, concrete information with warmth and curiosity.

➤ If they start repeating, summarize and ask if there's anything else, turn to another topic, or ask a question to elicit new information.

➤ **Refrain from discussing solutions.** It can be tempting but it works better if they fully explore different aspects of the situation before they start problem-solving. Note down any ideas to return to later.

**3.8
IMPARTIAL EMPATHY**

• *This has really been tough for everyone!*

• *That meant a lot to you.*

• *You've both had a really hard time.*

• *That kind of thing can be very painful.*

• *Thank you for going into those details.*

• *Take your time.*

• *So that was a huge loss!*

Note: Mean what you say (or don't say anything), say it warmly and respectfully, and keep it low-key.

[See also page 65.]

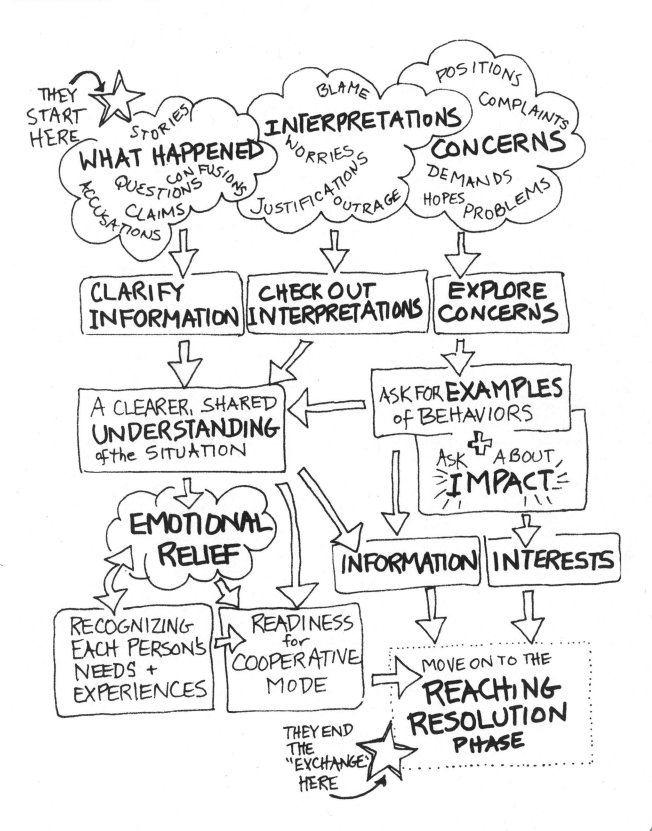

The Exchange: Task & flow

The sketch on page 41 outlines how the tasks of the Exchange connect to each other. All those arrows! Yes, it's a highly interactive, intertwined conversation. There is no set sequence, and participants usually bounce from one topic to another, with the mediators following their lead. However, eventually they need to cover the bases for each main concern: information, interpretations, "examples + impacts," and interests.

▶ To start, invite questions and responses

After the Listening go-round, participants usually launch into their own questions about facts ("What happened?") and motives ("Why did you do that?"). This is great, let it roll!

If they don't start talking spontaneously, invite them to respond to what they've heard:

> *Do either of you have a question for the other?*
>
> *Jane, I asked you to hold a thought a minute ago, would you like to talk about that now?*
>
> *I'm sure you have some questions, and I have some too.*

▶ Orient yourself to their context

Your background questions orient everyone to the broader context, and can sometimes spark a cooperative conversation. If they don't know each other well, the other party may need the information, too. Useful questions:

➤ **Ask for any information you need to follow the thread of their narrative.** Don't be shy: if you don't understand what they mean, you can't help them. Convey interest and curiosity; don't interrogate.

➤ **Ask for facts they will probably agree about.** Save probing questions about feelings, "what happened," and hot topics till later.

➤ **Ask for information which they can explain together**, such as drawing an organizational chart, putting together a timeline, looking at any photographs they brought. [**See sidebar and page 132.**]

Throughout the mediation, you can go back to these kinds of neutral, contextualizing questions to cool down or redirect conversation.

3.9
QUESTIONS ABOUT CONTEXT

- *Can you lay out the sequence of events for me?*

- *How long have you been working together?*

- *Would you sketch the layout of your office?*

- *I'm not clear about who owns each property.*

- *What are your staff meetings like?*

- *What's your usual schedule/process?*

- *How long is a board term?*

- *I'm a bit confused. Can you explain who works which shift?*

- *How often has this happened?*

Clarify information

▶ What information to look for

Concentrate on information that will move them towards resolution. Try to minimize the time they spend on information that serves to assign blame, that is second-hand, or that goes into repetitive detail. Useful information to look for:

- **The situation.** What happened, context, concerns, behaviors, impact.

- **Interests.** What do people want and need? Why do they care?

- **Facts that could help in problem-solving.** What is the standard process? Who is in charge of this piece? What's the deadline?

- **People's emotions and thoughts** about that information—reactions, stresses, interpretations, prejudices, assumptions, world-view.

- **People skills,** how parties interact with each other.

▶ Clear up misinformation, fill gaps

Quite often, participants discover significant misunderstandings about events, especially about the other parties' reasons for behaving as they did.

➤ **Experiences & choices.** Invite them to talk about how they personally experienced pivotal events and what choices they made.

➤ **Questions.** Encourage them to ask each other about any behavior that puzzled or upset them.

When the "truth" will not come out

Participants often respond to the other parties' "truths" with objections, disbelief, or fury. How to deal with irreconcilable accounts?

➤ **No persuading!** Caution—you are trying to get clearer and more specific information on the table, not trying to convince anyone to believe or trust what the other party says.

➤ **When they clash over facts or interpretations,** explain that they don't need to agree on what happened in order to move forward. It's normal for people to have different memories about the same incident. In any case, mediation can't determine whose version is "right."

➤ **Instead, ask about information that will help them decide** what to do next. [See page 151.]

Check out interpretations

⇛ Notice interpretations, assumptions

Participants often present their interpretations and assumptions as facts.

- **Generalizations about character**, i.e., jumping from "This is what William did." ➡ to "William is incompetent and unprofessional."

- **Generalizations about the situation**, "If you'd just do X, the problem would be solved." "This is hopeless, they'll never change." "The whole office is mad at you, it's not just me."

- **Worries (predictions).** "If William keeps the bull terrier, the landlord will throw us out." "If I don't agree to this, Jane will fire me."

- **Mind-reads.** Assumptions about what other people think, feel, or intend, e.g., jumping from "This is what William did" ➡ to "William despises us, he did this on purpose to get revenge."

⇛ Bring them back to first-hand information

➢ **Interrupt hearsay (speaking for others).** "The others don't trust you either." "He knows perfectly well that that's not true!" [**See sidebar 3.10.**]

➢ **Stop to check out mind-reads.**

> [With the speaker] *Ollie, what specifically did Colleen* **do** *that leads you to that conclusion?*

> [With the other person] *Ollie, let's take a minute and check that out. Colleen, would you like to explain what you were thinking at the time? What was your intention?*

➢ **Redirect accusatory questions or attacks** by asking the person to talk first about the impact on themselves. Reflect back, then restate their initial accusation as a request for information. [**See sidebar 3.11.**]

➢ **When they express worries,** ask:

> *If that actually happens, what might the consequences be for you?*

> *What experiences lead you to predict that will happen?*

**3.10
REDIRECTING
TO FIRST-HAND
INFORMATION**

- *Let's check with Ivan, since he was there that day.*

- *Could you tell us more about how YOU felt after that argument?*

- *Since Ellen isn't here, let's look at what YOU want to change.*

**3.11
REDIRECTING
ACCUSATIONS**

Wanda: "Why the hell did you…?"

➤ *Wanda, before Sophie answers that, could you talk about why that action upset you?* [Wanda explains….]

➤ *So you felt that your authority was undermined, and you'd like to know what Sophie was thinking when she did that?* [Wanda nods. Attention turns to Sophie.]

Listen for their concerns

▶ Concerns ➡ information and interests

In exploring each of a participant's concerns, mediators focus on getting specific *examples* of the behavior which troubles them, and the *impact* on them of that behavior. This grounds discussion in observed reality, and uncovers practical information for developing options later on. Asking for examples and impact helps bring each person's most troubling concerns to the surface. From these, the mediators distill the parties' interests and priorities, which will become the basis for evaluating options in the Reaching Resolution phase of the mediation.

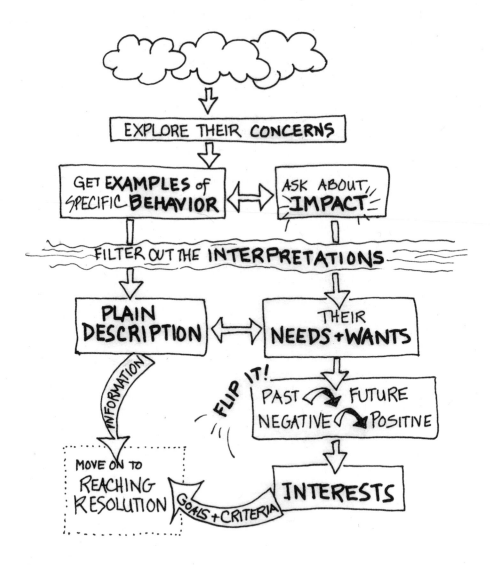

3.12
ELICITING KEY EXAMPLES

- *What was it she did that made you angry?*

- *Can you give us an example of what Vince did that leads you to call him lazy?*

- *Could you describe one key instance that illustrates the lateness problem?*

- *Is there a particular memory that sticks in your mind, or an incident you'd like to clear up?*

- *When you say you don't trust her, what's something she did that got you feeing that way?*

- *Could you tell us about one time when lack of communication created a problem?*

Example + impact

As the previous page illustrates, throughout the mediation, the mediator repeatedly steers conversations towards *examples* and *impact*. This can help keep the parties out of the swamp of positions and accusations. And it is particularly valuable in drawing out information and interests.

▶ Ask for an example of behavior

Problems are often presented indirectly as demands, attacks, or generalizations. ("I want her to apologize." "You stole it, don't lie!" "She *always* gets her way.") These show-stoppers can shut down or blow up a discussion. How can you move them towards "plain description"?

➤ Acknowledge the feeling they're conveying [**see page 101**], then ask for an example of something the other person said or did (or didn't do) that illustrates what they're concerned about. [**See sidebar 3.12.**]

➤ Focus conversation on examples of behavior—stripped of interpretation—to get underneath accusations and name-calling to more useful, less inflammatory information.

➤ If they cite several examples of the same kind of behavior with the same kind of impact, ask them to pick just one instance, and to describe it in detail.

▶ Ask about impact

Talking about impact—"Here's how his behavior affected me!"—gets to the core of what people want out of mediation. It brings the focus back to first-person direct experience, and can soften the other's sympathies.

Goal: A "plain description" of facts and needs

For each concern, keep asking for further specifics about behavior and impact until you have enough information to reflect back their facts and needs, minus the emotional charge. In effect, you're "translating" their account into neutral language so it can be heard by the other party:

> *So each time the alarm goes off, it delays you by two hours, which is hard because you have to leave by 5:30 to get to the daycare center before it closes?*

You've explored enough when your "translation" can provide:

✓ A neutrally worded but still accurate description everyone can hear without feeling put down, overlooked, or misunderstood.

✓ A level of factual detail concrete enough to help find a solution. [**See pages 152–53.**]

✓ Confirmation that you have fully captured the person's concern.

• *How did that affect you?*

• *How did you feel when X happened?*

• *When the deposits are delayed, how does that impact your business?*

• *It sounds like you've incurred some expenses…?*

• *Can you tell us why you feel strongly about this?*

• *What have been the personal consequences for you?*

• *You said X upset you—could you say more about that?*

Restate their interests

What's an interest?

An interest is a need or want that motivates a person's actions, something that they seek to protect or gain, something they care about. [**See also pages 145–48.**]

Mediation concentrates on interests that:

✓ Motivate participants' behavior—both at the table and in the future.

✓ Describe a positive state the participant hopes for (= need fulfilled).

✓ Can potentially be resolved through actions participants can take themselves.

Flip it!—What outcome *do* they want?

What they **don't** like **now** suggests what they **do** want in the **future**. "Flip" their account of yesterday's negative impact by inferring how they want tomorrow to be. For example, instead of reflecting back, "You don't like the room because it's too dark," say, *So you'd like the room to be well lit?*

Current negatives ➡ Positive wish for the future

By "positive," we don't mean rosy or ideal, but rather a satisfactory real-life situation they can create. Not every interest can be worded positively—but give it a try. Note too that the mediator doesn't get into WHO should light the room or HOW. Save that discussion for the Reaching Resolution phase. [**See page 154.**]

Restate the interest "cleanly"

You now have a final interest you can summarize, wording it to be:

✓ **Outcome-focused**—it's about what's wanted in the future; it doesn't just restate the problem.

✓ **Non-partisan**—It doesn't imply that one party's view or needs are more legitimate than another's. It's about the person whose interest it is, not about how they want the other party to behave or think. Where possible, don't *mention* the other party.

✓ **Non-judgmental**—it contains no words implying right, wrong, blame, or "shoulds." It uses tactful, neutral, non-inflammatory language.

✓ **Reasonable**—their need or goal sounds reasonable, legitimate (if possible!).

[**See also pages 154–56.**]

3.14
RESTATING INTERESTS

- *So Nancy, you want your annual review to be primarily based on your set goals and your job description?*

- *It sounds like you both want a new customer database that is simpler to use and can break out information needed by Marketing and Customer Service?*

- *Alice, you need some personal space for a while, setting up some indirect way to communicate with Bob when needed?*

- *Marvin, you'd like the division of assets to take your volunteer contributions into account, is that right?*

Note other relevant interests

▶ Highlight shared interests

Bring out any shared interests you notice.

> *It seems like you all want a practical workspace that also presents a good image to clients.*

> *Everyone wants Tommy to be able to live independently.*

Broad interests and goals like these help people reconnect with each other—we want similar things!—and widen the number of potential solutions, e.g., there are several ways to construct a practical workplace that feels good to clients, and to support Tommy's independence. [**See page 110.**]

▶ Interests the current situation meets now

The participants have probably been talking about what interests are *not* being met. However, even in the most distressing situation, the status quo may support some key interests that everyone can see as legitimate.

Maybe the technicians are communicating poorly with management because they enjoy their autonomy. Maybe Elaine arrives late because she has a second job that's crucial to her career plans. Maybe Nate has been contributing money rather than time to his family because he doesn't get along with his parents.

Once they move into the Reaching Resolution phase, proposed changes will need to remain responsive to these interests also. Otherwise their agreement may create a new set of problems, or people may revert to previous behaviors.

> ➤ People will usually spontaneously explain what leads them to do things that others say are having a negative impact. Help them translate these explanations into statements about their interests.

> ➤ If they don't seek to justify their actions, ask them questions to explore what interests their behaviors may be supporting. Do it tactfully, by asking in a tone that tells them you assume—it's not even open to question!—they are doing the behavior for a legitimate reason. Use acknowledging to show empathy. [**See page 101.**]

> ➤ After they've thoroughly explored what's not working, ask what, if anything, is working okay about the current situation. Explain it's "so we don't throw the baby out with the bathwater." Avoid giving the impression you want them to "look on the bright side." Then ask them for a single example that illustrates the benefits it provides to get at the interests that all agree need protecting. [**See page 46.**]

**3.15
WHAT'S WORKING?**

• *What's working okay that you want to continue?*

• *Has anything changed lately that is working better?*

• *Before you discuss revising the regulations—are there useful aspects that you would like to keep?*

• *It sounds like the current financial arrangements are okay with both of you?*

• *You said your son likes the visitation schedule as it is— what are you thinking he likes about it?*

Encourage empathy and reconciliation

Mediation's methodical information-sharing can gradually ease people's emotional state and give them hope that there's a way out. They may begin to acknowledge the other party's needs — maybe even feel some compassion — and be willing to work together to find a fair resolution.

What else can the mediator do to create the conditions for empathy and reconciliation?

➤ **Be gentle with their pain.** If they fall into silence, hold it with calm and warmth. If someone cries, pass the tissues and either wait quietly or ask if they'd like to take a break. Acknowledge, help them find words [**See sidebar 3.8, page 40.**]:

> *You seem really sad about the breakup…*

> *It's clearly been a tough time for everybody.*

➤ **Ask about positive things they share or care about**, what's working now, previous good times. For some, children can be a soft spot.

> *So you both enjoy playing on the company soccer team.*

> *You've known her daughter since she was a baby?*

➤ **If someone asks for an apology**, do not turn expectantly to the other party. The receiver is likely to discount any apology that appears forced. Instead treat it as you would any other demand — find out what need it expresses: *If Kim apologized, how would that change things for you?*

➤ If and only if the moment seems right, invite them to express any regrets or appreciations they'd like to share. [**See sidebar 4.6, page 70.**]

▶ The turning-point phenomenon

In mediations involving parties who previously had a close relationship but became estranged, mediators sometimes witness a marked emotional shift, which we call the "turning point." It may happen after someone makes an apology, or offers a concession or a kind word. There may be a pause. Then, like water rushing through a breach in the dam, there may come a mutual outpouring of personal sharing, ideas and offers.

Often the spurt of energy propels them into spontaneous problem-solving. Sit back and let them go to it. (Later, you can loop back to check whether there's anything else they still need to address, using a Topic List. [**See page 50.**]) This dramatic U-turn is not necessary for reaching resolution, and not something a mediator can make happen. But you can be ready to recognize and make room for it when it does.

Transition to Reaching Resolution

▶ Are they ready to end the Exchange?

Whether or not participants' adversarial stances have softened in the course of the Exchange, eventually you'll start to feel it may be time for the parties to end this phase and move into Reaching Resolution. How to test their readiness? Propose a Topic List. [See page 59.]

If they tell you the Topic List is complete, that means they are ready to make the transition to Reaching Resolution. So proposing one is a great way to find out if you still need to continue with the Exchange. You will proceed to joint problem-solving ONLY if they tell you the Topic List is complete.

If they say the Topic List isn't complete, ask them what's missing. That will tell you what they still have to talk about in the Exchange. Once you've understood the interests involved, add what's missing to the Topic List and propose it again.

This means, in practice, that *proposing* a Topic List is *also a tool for the Exchange.* Like any summary, when it's not complete, that helps the parties (and you) see more clearly what else they still need to talk about. So you can't go wrong trying it.

You might decide to try a Topic List for any of these reasons:

➤ **They're sounding more cooperative and empathetic,** talking less about the concerns and worries, and more about solutions. They may even directly say that they'd like to start problem-solving.

➤ **You think they've finished the work of the Exchange.**

✓ Just rehashing concerns and needs they've already expressed.

✓ No big information gaps.

✓ No misunderstandings or mind-reads that need clearing up.

✓ The concerns and needs they care about have been translated into *interests*—those positive, tactful, "reasonable" wishes for the future that any agreement will have to satisfy if it is to resolve the situation.

➤ **You wonder if they are tiring,** or when they'll ever be finished with the Exchange, and you want to test whether they're ready for problem-solving.

Answer: Propose a Topic List, ask if it's complete—and find out!

Separate Conversations

SUMMARY:
SEPARATE CONVERSATIONS

- **Hold them any time during the mediation**

- **Touch base with *each* party**

- **Stay impartial**

- **Stick to your time frame**

- **Keep the conversation confidential**

- **Don't do their work for them!**

▶ Purpose

Separate Conversations are private meetings with each party, during or between sessions. (See Chapter 2 for pre-mediation conversations.)

Separate Conversations are a place for strategizing and coaching—to help parties figure out how to talk about touchy subjects, or decide whether to share information that could cause trouble (e.g., disclosing illegal behavior, adultery, etc.). They can also give participants space to think through options without having to watch what they're saying or doing at the table.

When parties have (or have had) a close personal relationship, a Separate Conversation can be crucial, if only to check whether there's anything else a participant wants you to know—background information, fears, or painful memories they are hesitant to bring out at the table.

Some mediators are wary of breaking momentum, making each party wait around, or diminishing their trust in each other ("What's that person saying about me in there?"). These are cautions to consider when you decide whether to hold Separate Conversations.

Participants are usually happy to talk at length when alone with an attentive mediator. The challenge is to keep the Separate Conversation brief (!), and get them back at the table together quickly.

Uses for Separate Conversations

SUPPORT THE PEOPLE

- Give them time to cool off, pull themselves together, or let off steam (sometimes *a lot* of steam!).

- Hear what a shy or fearful person has to say.

- Help people think through what they want, and how to say it so the other party understands.

- Discuss problematic assumptions, interpretations, expectations.

- Rehearse how they might bring up a touchy issue.

- Show more caring than you can at the table (being careful about impartiality).

FACILITATE THE PROCESS

- Regroup! Change gears! Consult and get information to figure out where the conversation should go next.

- Explore the interests and feelings driving behaviors that make participation more difficult (attacking, withdrawing, name-calling, stonewalling, etc.).

- Slow the process down, give everyone time to think.

- Explore what they want from the mediation or what alternatives they have if they quit mediation.

- Help members of one party work out their internal divisions so they can participate more effectively.

SOLVE A PROBLEM

- Receive private information, check that you fully understand what they want, raise aspects that they seem reluctant to talk about at the table.

- Be a sounding board for ideas, strategies, options.

- Explore ways to "unstick" a discussion or impasse—reframe the topic, expand the range of options, locate resources, etc.

- Discuss the potential consequences of various choices.

- Think through offers they might want to make, consider the other party's offers or requests, explore hypothetical trade-offs (*What might you feel comfortable offering them, what would you want in return?*).

- Test the workability and durability of their agreement.

Breaking for Separate Conversations

▶ Taking a regular free-time break

Taking a break can be helpful even if you don't have Separate Conversations. This gives the parties—and mediators—time to stretch, clear their heads, recover from an emotional moment, or check their messages. Co-mediators can confer with each other; participants can confer with others in their party. And if a session will run longer than 2–2½ hours, a break is essential.

Remember to take your notes with you if you leave the table!!!

▶ Breaking for Separate Conversations

➤ **Don't make it a big deal.** Break for Separate Conversations in a matter-of-fact tone, without giving a reason. You don't want to imply they've been "bad" or the mediation is "difficult."

> *Let's take a break now, and we'll touch base with each of you one-on-one.*

➤ **Be clear in your own mind about what you want to discuss** with each party so you can keep it short and focused. If you just want a general check-in, tell them that. *I just wanted to check in and see how things are going from your point of view.*

➤ **Tell the waiting party how long you will be.** If you're running longer than expected, let them know. You can also suggest a topic that parties can think about or make notes on while they are waiting.

➤ **Always meet with each party** to retain their trust in your impartiality. (You can always start with a general "checking-in" question when meeting with someone for balance only.)

➤ **Mediator teams have a choice.** Splitting up so each mediator talks with one of the parties may be a time-saver, though mediators must then take time to fill each other in before reconvening. It may even be necessary—if one party seems in no condition to be left alone, or is on the verge of walking out. On the other hand, if the mediation team meets with each party in turn, the mediators all have access to the same information, and there's no implication that each mediator "belongs" to one party.

Separate Conversations: Template

**3.16
SEPARATE
CONVERSATIONS
TEMPLATE**

1. Assure them of confidentiality.

2. *We wanted to talk with you about* _____.

3. Be understanding but impartial.

4. Stick to your time frame.

5. *When we go back to the table,* _____.

1. Assure them of confidentiality.

I will not report anything you say without your permission.

2. Tell them what you want to discuss.

We wanted to talk to you about _____.

How I can make this session useful for you?

What's your sense of how things are going?

Is there anything important you haven't brought up at the table yet?

Aim for fresh information, not rehashing!

3. Be understanding but impartial.

You can tell them you know the situation is hard, that it can be difficult to know what to do. Be careful not appear to support their position, accept their assessment of the situation, or become their advocate. Participants have been known to quote the mediator back at the table: "The *mediator* agrees with me that your demands are unrealistic...."

4. Stick to your time frame.

Set a time frame for yourself, and don't keep the other parties waiting too long. People *love* to have the private ear of the mediators!

5. *When we go back to the table....*

End by asking *them* to summarize what they plan to do or say when everyone returns to the table (as opposed to summarizing it for them) — for example, that they will make an offer of X, or raise a thorny issue.

Also confirm what *you* will say or do, if relevant. In principle, you want them to do the talking, but if you and they decide you should say something — either to the other party in private or back at the table — make clear to all participants that you are doing so with express permission.

THE MEDIATION SESSION PART II: REACHING RESOLUTION

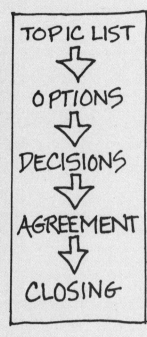

REACHING RESOLUTION

TOPIC LIST
⇩
OPTIONS
⇩
DECISIONS
⇩
AGREEMENT
⇩
CLOSING

THE PROCESS

4

Reaching Resolution

▶ Purpose: Planning for the future

Reaching Resolution is the future-oriented phase of the mediation:

- What steps might meet all parties' interests?

- Which of those steps are they willing and able to take?

- How do they want to relate to each other—if at all?

- What recompense or repair might make that more likely?

- If they want to rebuild trust, what will it take?

This part of the mediation tends to be both more structured and more creative than the Exchange, as the parties work topic by topic to find feasible options that will meet their interests, to develop tentative points of agreement—and then to put it all together.

For each topic, the participants generate some general ideas ("Ben could buy out the other family members' shares"), then work through a series of small decisions, from *Which idea seems most promising?* through testing it against criteria (*Would this meet both your interests? Can it be done?*), exploring how to improve it, and finally, getting down to the fine-grain terms—who will do what by when and how. ("Ben agrees to put $64K into escrow with Smeal, Esq., by 5 PM on March 31st.")

On the emotional side, as possibilities open up, the parties often start to feel lighter and more energized. Thinking together toward a common goal tends to forge a cooperative attitude that helps people (re)build their relationships and sustain their commitments to each other. In the end, it may not even be *what* they decide, but the fact they decided it *together*, that makes for a lasting resolution.

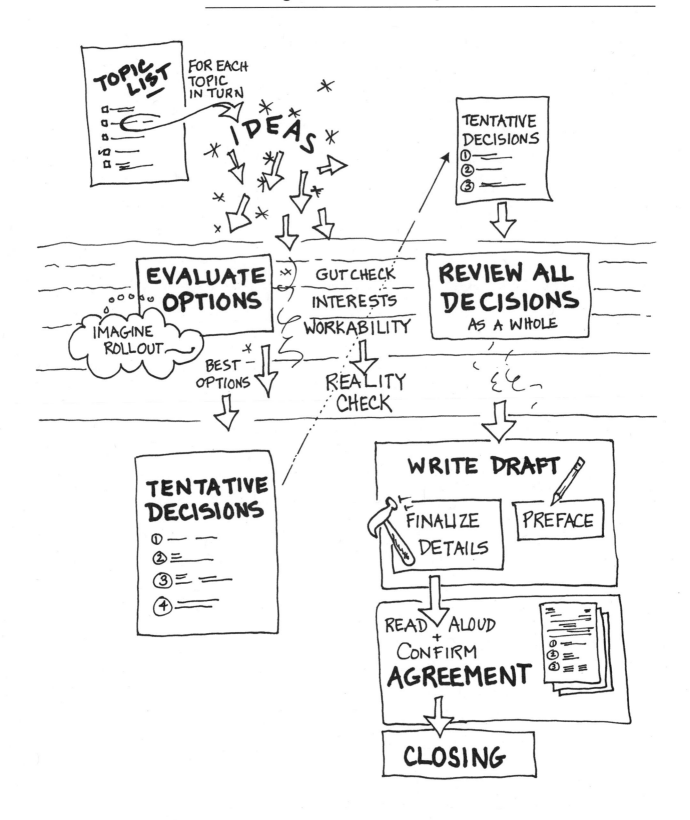

Topic List

SUMMARY: TOPIC LIST

1. **Group related concerns into a few topics**

2. **Word them for joint problem-solving**

3. **Discuss and get approval of the list as a whole:**

   - **Covers everything?**

   - **Clear and acceptable wording?**

▶ Purpose: What's the work ahead of us?

Once the parties have put their concerns on the table, and you have helped them translate those concerns into tactfully worded, future-focused interests [**see page 47**], the next step is to organize those reframed concerns into a tentative list of all the topics they need to discuss and decide. The list is adjusted and refined until all parties agree it's accurate and complete. Like a meeting agenda, the Topic List structures the discussion, reassuring the parties that everything will be covered in its turn.

You'll want to work towards a tentative Topic List as you take notes during the Exchange. If there are many topics, you may want to call a break to give yourself time to draft it. Don't worry if the categories aren't obvious, or are difficult to word: offer the parties your best guess, then get their input to refine the list until all can approve it.

A place for each concern and interest

Topics are like boxes for organizing your closet. There may be several sensible ways to sort items — shirts in one box, socks in another, or winter clothes in one, summer clothes in another. The same goes for sorting the parties' concerns into clusters that make sense to discuss and resolve together. There may be different ways of combining concerns into topics, but it's most important to make sure every concern is addressed somewhere (even if it is a topic all by itself).

4.1 SAMPLE TOPIC LIST

It sounds like these are the things you need to decide to resolve the situation:

✓ *Back rent: How to handle payments for last March and April.*

✓ *Stove repair: Quality, who pays, who will do it, time frame.*

✓ *Landlord access: How and when can he access the apartment?*

✓ *Communication: How you want to deal with future problems, if they come up.*

✓ *Lease: Whether to renew the lease.*

Have I included everything?

Topic List: Why it is crucial

Getting a Topic List approved may only take a few minutes, but it is often crucial for reaching resolution— and not only because it helps organize the problem-solving process. It also has a remarkable ability to shift people into a more relaxed, hopeful, cooperative, and creative frame of mind.

Before approving a Topic List:

➤ Participants tend to feel the dispute is chaotic, fuzzy-edged, limitless, and everlasting.

➤ They worry they'll forget to press some of their concerns and needs. And they worry you will too.

➤ Even worse, they fear they will make concessions only to find that the other parties keep bringing up new concerns and needs.

All these uncertainties and worries make it hard for people to relax enough to be creative and flexible, and stay focused on any one subset of concerns long enough to resolve it.

After approving a Topic List:

➤ Participants tend to relax and let go somewhat. They don't have to worry anything will be forgotten.

➤ Just as important, they've heard the other parties agree that it covers everything. They don't have to worry that the complaints and demands from those quarters will be endless.

➤ They see that the dispute is well-defined and limited in scope, with a clear end in sight, and that the problem–solving process will be orderly.

As a result, participants tend to relax some and reorient with new energy toward resolution. It's like having been lost without a map, then suddenly finding a map in hand.

The Topic List's "magic" works *only* if all are comfortable with the wording and agree it's accurate and complete. So it's very important to keep adjusting the list until they can all do a gut check and say, "You've got it!"

Sometimes participants will spontaneously start working on solutions before you propose a Topic List. Let them roll, but if they get stuck, that's your cue to back up and get a Topic List approved.

New mediators find it takes practice to work up a Topic List while the parties are talking. At first, try giving them a brief break while you think through how to organize it. It will be well worth their time.

Topic List: Drafting

▶ Characteristics of a useful topic

✓ It's one that must be addressed if they want the conflict resolved.

✓ Participants can take action to improve it.

✓ It does not require a change of values, feelings, or belief. Thus, "Respect each other more" is not a topic. "How can we create a more respectful atmosphere?" might be.

✓ If one party has sole authority to decide a topic (e.g., a manager's policies, a teacher's grading plan), they are open to seeking solutions that meet all parties' interests.

✓ It suggests a goal that might link divergent interests. Manager Polly may not care that salesclerk Justine has family problems. But she may care if it means Justine is getting to work late. *How to get the store ready to open at 10am* allows discussion of how to accommodate or support Justine and still meet Polly's needs.

How broad or narrow should a topic be?

➤ **Look for a useful level of specificity**—broad enough that they can imagine several options, yet focused enough that they don't try to untangle everything at once. Thus, *How sales clerks can handle difficult customers* lays a stronger foundation for mutual problem-solving than the general "How to improve communication." [**See page 159.**]

➤ **Aim for five to seven topics at the most.** A short list is easier to remember and less daunting.

➤ **Use subtopics.** To keep the list a manageable size, you can define a topic as a broad direction, wording it either as:

1. A value or need. *How to give your Mom the best care.*

2. An action goal. *Moving your Mom to a good nursing home soon.*

Then list subtopics they need to address to get there.

Add these topics to the List

Whether or not the parties bring them up, these topics often belong at the end of the Topic List. Addressing them brings finality to the agreement.

✓ How to communicate should problems or tensions arise again.

✓ How to handle any pending proceedings, such as grievance, performance review, or lawsuit.

Topic List: Wording

▶ Word the topics for joint problem-solving

Word topics as a question to resolve: "*How to divide the income,*" "*What membership criteria to institute.*"

➤ **Tactful & positive.** Follow the guidelines for wording topics. [**See pages 155, 157.**]

➤ **Add a short-hand label** you can later use to refer to each topic. Remember, it's a *list*! [**See sidebar 4.1, page 59.**]

➤ **Explain what a larger topic encompasses.**

> *The second topic is, "How to assign Co-op member hours." That includes how to credit volunteer time, and also what to do about less popular tasks.*

▶ Discuss and confirm the Topic List

➤ **Read your list out loud and post it where all can see it**, if possible.

➤ **Ask, *Does this list cover everything you need to talk about to resolve the situation?*** (Note that you do mean "everything" they think needs addressing, not just the "main topics," or "key concerns.")

➤ **Ask, *Is anything missing?*** This is the gut-check question. If they want to add a concern or place it under a different topic, you may need to go back into the Exchange mode briefly to clarify the interests involved or figure out where it should go.

➤ **Ask if the wording is okay, and adjust it together to be tactful and clear.** If someone feels that the topic is fuzzy, biased, judgmental, or implies a particular solution, they'll be uncomfortable negotiating it.

➤ **Review timing.** Estimate how many topics you think they can realistically hope to cover today (remembering to leave time for closing). Discuss priorities and whether they will want to schedule another session.

➤ **Suggest a topic to start with.** If there isn't a logical sequence where X is needed to lay the ground for Y, you can suggest one they care most about, or one that's fairly easy and might give a sense of accomplishment to build on. Be flexible if they prefer starting with something different.

Note: If a new topic surfaces, it is likely to be something important that a participant has been holding back. Take the time for everyone to listen and discuss what the person is saying.

Midpoint check-in

▶ Check-in & encouragement

This can be a good moment to check how they are feeling about the mediation process: discouraged? eager? skeptical? tired?

To launch problem-solving on an upbeat note, you might recap the views and goals they share and anything they've decided on already. Express your confidence in their ability to work their way through to an agreement.

This can also be a good time to take a break, particularly if you want them to have some time to think and consult before discussing options. You may also want to do a time-check. How much of their Topic List can they hope to get through today? If they may need another session, it's good to mention that now so they don't feel let down at the end of this one.

Options

4.2 QUESTIONS TO ELICIT IDEAS

- *What else might work?*

- *What can you offer that you think the other party might be able to live with?*

- *Gina has mentioned a few ideas. What are some of yours?*

- *Let's make a quick idea list here—even ones that seem unrealistic…*

- *What's already working well that you could build on?*

- *Imagine you are getting along well again…. what does life look like?*

- *If you had all the money and time you needed, what solutions might you try?*

- *Ideally, what do you hope Topic X will look like in the future?*

SUMMARY: OPTIONS FOR EACH TOPIC

1. **Get several ideas on the table**

2. **Imagine how options might play out:**

   - **Gut response**

   - **Fits with interests?**

   - **Workability**

3. **Reality testing**

4. **Note tentative agreements**

▶ Purpose: Find acceptable options

The Options phase sorts through ideas and options to find acceptable solutions for each topic on the Topic List.

If they have already rejected customary solutions or the other party's proposals, they will need to come up with new ideas. Mediators are especially useful at this point, because parties can have a hard time being inventive and flexible if they are still in adversarial mode. A respectful or playful approach can help reduce the risk of exploring fresh ideas.

Insist that they come up with several ideas before evaluating any. Then help them explore how the most promising ideas might be adjusted or combined to meet their interests, to test that they're workable, to make sure they feel right.

This approach can help unlock the parties from the typical zero-sum mindset of human beings in conflict—that anything my adversary wants must be bad for me; that anything I like they'll automatically oppose; that agreement must mean compromise and concessions.

Options: Together come up with ideas

▶ Get several ideas on the table

For each topic on the list in turn, walk them through a process to help them come up with options:

1. **Name the selected topic,** and/or write it at the top of the board or chart.

2. **Ask them to think of several ideas without discussing** any of them yet. If the mood is cooperative, you might want to try a full brainstorm. [**See page 158.**]

3. **Write each idea down without comment,** unless you need to clarify what they mean.

➤ **Don't let them start evaluating.** It can make people cautious or defensive, which gets in the way of frank and creative thinking.

➤ **Keep your opinion hidden,** even when it is positive (e.g., don't exclaim, "great idea!" or appear to be thinking over the value of their idea).

➤ **If conversation strays a bit, that's fine.** The creative mind is not linear. Keep side lists for ideas relevant to other topics.

➤ **Deflect darts lightly.** When someone says, "If Fred would just leave town, it would solve everything!" quietly put "move away" on the list. If it's a passing taunt to ignite a hot response, you may choose to keep moving. If it signals a surprisingly strong feeling, it's best to stop and explore what's going on.

➤ **Stuck?** For suggestions about types of solutions, especially when trust is low or it is hard to meet all parties' interests, see pages 163–64 and 166–67. You could also change topics, take a think-time break, or hold Separate Conversations.

▶ Imagine how options might play out

1. **Choose.** Ask the group to pick out promising ideas, and decide which one to look at first.

2. **Clarify.** Ask whether the person who suggested it wants to say more about what they had in mind.

3. **Imagine.** Ask everyone to picture how that option might play out.

Discussion will usually flow, without much facilitation, like this:

Gut response ➡ Does it meet our interests? ➡ Is it workable?

as laid out on the next page. Hearing *why* they like or reject various options helps everyone get clearer about their own and other participants' interests and priorities, and what practical obstacles they face.

Options: Gut, interests, workability

GUT RESPONSE?

- *What's your first response to this idea?*
- *What makes you feel that way?*
- *What is it that you (don't) like about it?*

FIT WITH INTERESTS?

- *What might make this suggestion more appealing?*
- *Does this meet your concern about _____?*
- *How well does this option meet both Rick's need for _____ and Erica's need for _____?*
- *How might you all adjust this idea to address Ranya's concern?*
- *Does this help get the organization where you want it to be in a year's time?*

WORKABLE?

- *What would it take to make this work?*
- *Can you picture yourself doing so?*
- *What are ways you can get around this (objection, drawback)?*
- *What support, resources, and information will you need?*
- *Might it create other difficulties?*

Use this testing sequence for each serious option (and again later for reviewing the whole agreement). If someone reacts negatively to an idea, probe a bit, but don't belabor it—*OK, let's move on to another suggestion.*

1. **Gut response** is a quick assessment of whether the idea is promising or objectionable—is it worth discussing further?

2. **Fit with interests** means, "Does this move them towards creating the kind of situation or future they want?"

3. **Workability** means whether the option is doable, whether they will be able to make it work.

Options: Reality testing

▶ Testing best options: obstacles, what-ifs

Once participants have settled on an option they think will work, review it more carefully. Ask them to visualize the proposed solution again, this time on the lookout for potential obstacles—resources, support, access, etc. [**See page 160.**] Are there any "what if" circumstances that might derail their plans? [**See page 165.**]

The mediator's agent-of-reality role

Part of the mediator's role is helping people make plans that are grounded in reality. Review the option in your own mind too. Then raise issues you think need attention. A tone of noncommittal curiosity can draw out thoughtful responses. [**See pages 105, 126.**]

➤ **Positives.** Does the solution build on people's strengths and resources? Does it respect them, and not imply blame and distrust?

➤ **Unintended consequences.** Even if this fixes problem X, might it make Y worse, or create new problems?

➤ **Potential roadblocks, glitches.** Have they thought through what to do about aspects they can't control? (Will their management accept this financial settlement? Can they make their teenagers stop talking to each other? What if it rains next weekend?)

➤ **Commitment.** Do they seem comfortable that this is the right direction, that it meets their goals and hopes? Or do you sense that they are in a hurry to settle? Have they given up on getting what they want?

Use your agent-of-reality questions sparingly, regretfully, sympathetically. Take care not to imply that their decision is a bad idea. Don't try to steer them—directly or indirectly—toward a choice you think is better or more obviously workable.

If the parties still think the option is workable, summarize it out loud and put it on the "tentative decisions" list.

**4.3
AGENT-OF-REALITY
QUESTIONS**

• *How easy will it be for you to do this?*

• *Are there aspects that might be hard for you to follow through on?*

• *Will your membership support this change?*

• *If you need to be done by August, what's the timetable to get there?*

• *How might this option affect your community?*

What-ifs

• *What might happen if _____?*

• *How will you handle _____?*

• *How will this work during the winter months?*

• *If Bob forgets to tell you, or you're delayed, would this plan still hold?*

[See also page 165.]

Decisions

SUMMARY: DECISIONS

1. **Review the agreement as a whole:**

   - **Fair, balanced**

   - **Satisfies key interests**

   - **Workable, lasting**

2. **Listen for hesitations**

3. **Agree on who will draft the final agreement**

▶ Purpose: Review the whole agreement

After they have worked through each topic on the Topic List, the participants review their list of tentative decisions as a whole package, and usually proceed to record them in a written agreement.

The mediator patiently double-checks that everyone's concerns have been addressed, clarifies details and ambiguities, and confirms that each person feels willing and able to follow through.

The process of writing a draft agreement interweaves with the process of review and decisions about details, even though they are explained sequentially in this chapter. See Chapter 8, "Solving the Problem," for more information about crafting solid agreements.

One cautionary note about decision fatigue. People can make only a limited number of decisions — even small ones like which soda they want to drink — before they start making hasty choices or shutting down and sticking with the status quo. Taking the time for a substantial break to refresh their minds, giving them something to eat, or postponing till the second session may in the end give them a stronger agreement.

Decisions: Gut, interests, workability

▶ Criteria for a durable agreement

If an agreement contains more than four decisions or so, take time to review it as a whole, using the same *gut* ➡ *interests* ➡ *workability* sequence as before.

➢ How well do the pieces of the agreement work together?

➢ What needs to be adjusted or added?

Participants may need a break to think things through or to consult others.

Gut check: Does it feel fair and balanced overall?

✓ Each party feels they are giving and receiving a fair deal. If they don't think it is "fair," are they willing to live with that imbalance?

✓ They believe they can reasonably carry out their promises.

✓ They feel that any compensation is in proportion to the damage done or the trade-offs they have made.

Interests: Does it address all their concerns?

✓ Interests of each participant, including **emotional** and **social needs**.

✓ Interests of stakeholders who are not at the table, including any referral source.

✓ Systemic problems they've identified that they want to address or accommodate in some way.

Workability: Is it likely to last?

✓ No loose ends, vague terms, or ambiguities.

✓ Keeping the agreement seems to be to each party's advantage.

✓ They have the resources and support they need to make it work.

✓ "What ifs," compromises, risks, contradictions, missing information, contingencies have been thoroughly discussed.

4.4
REVIEW QUESTIONS

• *Have we covered everything?*

• *Is there any piece of this you're uneasy with?*

• *Can you live with this over the long haul?*

• *Can you picture yourself doing this?*

• *Will it feel okay to tell your friends and family about this decision?*

• *Does anyone have unfinished business they want to bring up?*

• *Are you ready to put this in writing now?*

Decisions: Emotions, hesitations

4.5
CHECK FOR UNRESOLVED HURTS

• *Is there an experience you've had that makes you worry whether this agreement will work?*

• *Is there anything left that you want to say or ask each other before we finalize this?*

• *How are you feeling about your ability to work with each other on this?*

• *Sounds like you're a little hesitant?*

• *Is there anything in your previous experiences that might affect your feelings about _____? Your ability to _____?*

▶ Acknowledge losses, gains

Commitment is an emotional decision, not just a calculated one. No matter how good people feel about a reconciliation, they may also feel some sense of loss.

➤ **Hard choices.** Empathize with their anguish or dilemmas, being careful to stay outcome-neutral.

➤ **Losses** usually loom larger in people's minds than gains. Acknowledge what they are letting go.

➤ **Intangible gains.** Ask what they hope they might gain, including intangibles like peace of mind. Are the benefits worth the cost?

▶ Ease the pressure to agree

Are they are making hasty revisions in their hurry to agree and get out of there? Digging in their heels when others push them to agree?

➤ **Affirm that there's no obligation to reach an agreement.**

➤ **Check out your observations** privately or at the table:

> *Frieda, you said having autonomy in this project was critical, yet it seems this proposal isn't going to give you that. What's your thinking about this?*

▶ Last-minute wavering

Reassure them it's normal to feel some unease venturing into new territory: No agreement is entered into without hesitation. But if someone says they've changed their mind — even if they just express skepticism or seem reluctant — don't ignore them or try to talk them out of it. If there's a can of worms, better to open it now.

➤ **Thank them** for bringing it up. It shows they take commitment to an agreement seriously.

➤ **Ask what doesn't feel right**, what worries them. If it's a distressing memory or sore spot that hasn't been discussed, encourage them to describe it. Help them check any assumptions or mind-reads. [**See sidebar 4.6 and page 150.**]

> *It's clear you're both feeling some skepticism that the other person will follow through. How would you like to proceed?*

➤ If they decide not to come to agreement, **see page 168.**

Writing the Agreement

▶ Purpose: Commitment, clarity

Should they write down their agreement? Well, yes. A written document:

- Makes it more likely that their final agreement is specific, complete, and mutually understood.

- Confirms that everyone understands the promises they are making.

- Reinforces a sense of seriousness and commitment.

- Reminds people afterwards what exactly they agreed to, and may avert fresh arguments.

- Is tangible evidence that they accomplished something *together*, and marks a clear end to the mediation process.

Alternatives to a signed agreement

In some relationships or cultures, giving one's word is sufficient. A written document may feel too formal, suggesting a lack of trust and the fragility of their promises. People may also worry that they risk punitive action should the agreement fail. Often, calling it a "summary" or "notes" instead of an "agreement" resolves this concern. In addition, or instead, you may suggest:

➤ **A meaningful, ideally public, exchange** of money, gifts, apologies, or joint actions.

➤ **Other symbolic ways to mark reconciliation**, such as a handshake, a dinner, an announcement, or even just an exchange of contact information.

Agree who will draft the final agreement

➤ If they want you to write up the agreement, follow the drafting guidelines laid out on the next pages.

➤ If lawyers will be finalizing the document, title it a "Draft Memo of Understanding." In the header, write: "Parties' Draft for Lawyers' Review— Confidential," and the date.

➤ If you sign it, write that you're signing as a witness, not a party, and that your signature does not constitute approval or disapproval.

➤ Have the parties' sign a separate agreement with you affirming that they agree not to interpret anything you say or write as legal advice.

➤ Familiarize yourself with what counts as the "unauthorized practice of law" in your jurisdiction; if in doubt, get legal advice.

Writing the Agreement

Take great care with what goes on paper. As the only official record of the work done in the mediation, the agreement contains what people will most likely remember about the process as well as the outcome. Help them construct an agreement which is complete, accurate, and unambiguous.

▶ Preface: Context, goals, goodwill

Because they are reaching a resolution, not just an agreement, start the document by briefly describing the parties' mutual intentions and good will, and any overall principles, goals, or hopes they've expressed. This can also help motivate follow-through.

> *We four partners wish to sustain and grow our business in a spirit of amicable and open collaboration. In this context, we agree to the following:*

➤ **Use their language** as much as you can.

➤ **Visually separate the preface** from the points of agreement.

➤ **Word it as a shared hope or principle** rather than as a rule. You don't want them later accusing a party who raises a divergent viewpoint of being "uncollaborative" or "breaching the agreement."

4.6
SAMPLE PREFACES

- Everyone agrees that they want to get the WackyWidgets product to market within the year.

- The stakeholder representatives have worked for 3 months to draw up the following guidelines for the zoning board. Our recommendations are based on the following two principles: _____.

- All of us agree that Rita has done a wonderful job with the endowment fund.

- Walt and Olga agree that it is critically important for their children to have two active parents, and they agree to make parenting decisions based on this principle.

- Our families feel regret about what happened, and wish to make a fresh start. To help that happen, we agree to the following: _____.

Writing the Agreement: Specifics

▶ Details: Accurate, clear, and complete

➤ **Who, when, where, how, how much, deadlines, milestones.** The agreement needs to dot all the i's and cross all the t's. Simply writing "Ida Wrangle and the McBickers agree to rebuild the fence between their properties this summer." is asking for trouble. Glitches or disagreements may not show up until the fence posts are being put in. The sidebar illustrates a suitable level of detail.

➤ **Watch out for ambiguous words** that can be interpreted more than one way. (Will the other party think David did the "thorough" job he promised?) Down the line, differing interpretations can reignite disagreements. Make sure they are agreeing to the same thing! Start by flagging these:

- **Adjectives** are by nature subjective, not measurable, and therefore open to different interpretations (quiet, professional, sufficient, reasonable, neighborly, clean, respectful, punctual).

- **Non-specific times** pose the same problem (soon, as needed, often, when finished).

➤ **Keep the process moving.** Participants sometimes get restless trudging through all the details. Try to be efficient and good humored—they want to be *done.*

▶ Language: Tactful, familiar

➤ **Use the parties' wording**, as long as their language is neutral and clear. Avoid bureaucratic or legalistic terms (such as "prior to," "harassment," "pertaining," "grievance," "complainant"). If legal language is necessary, let the parties' lawyers be responsible for that.

➤ **Keep it neutral.** Watch for names, terms, and explanations that might seem linked to one side's viewpoint.

➤ **Avoid blame or criticism.** "George agrees to clean up ~~regularly from now on~~ the office every Tuesday." "Harold agrees to pay Paula $4500 for the damage ~~caused by his faulty installation~~."

➤ **Make it skimmable.** Number the main decisions, use bullet points or letters for subpoints. Keep sentences short, leave spaces between items.

4.7
SAMPLE OF SPECIFICS IN AN AGREEMENT

1. Ida Wrangle and the McBickers agree to build a 6-foot stockade fence 12 inches in from Ida's side of the property line.

2. Since Ida Wrangle will be the owner of the fence, she agrees to pay for materials and apply for a permit before June 8.

3. Bud McBicker agrees to construct the fence by July 30, and will email Ida by next Thursday about the cost of materials he needs to purchase.

4. If Ida has questions or concerns about the construction of the fence, she will email them to Bud before August 7.

For full sample agreements, see pages 171–72.

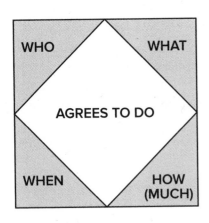

▶ Framing: Mutual, positive, doable

Mutual

➤ **Use the verb "agree,"** instead of "will." This underscores that the participants have *chosen* this decision: *Tim and Judy agree to meet every Thursday at 4 PM.*

➤ **Everyone gives and gains.** Avoid having six items that start with *Judy agrees to* _____ , and only one that starts with *Tim agrees to* _____ . Of course, if the agreement truly *is* lopsided, parties need to discuss it.

➤ **Record decisions as mutual** when you can: *George and Susan agree to* _____ . Or, *Susan and George agree that Susan will....*

Positive

➤ **Describe what the parties agree they WILL do**—rather than what they *won't* do or will stop doing—whenever you can. Thus, instead of "Karl agrees not to make purchases greater than $7,000 unless Regina gives written permission," you might write:

> *Karl agrees to email Regina for approval at least 4 workdays before he makes purchases over $7,000. Regina agrees to email him her decision within 2 workdays of receiving his email.*

Doable

➤ **Break large-scale or complex actions into sub-steps** with milestones. Encourage them not to promise more than they feel they can deliver.

➤ **Provide for contingencies & uncertainties.** Use fallbacks to protect against external factors which may undermine the agreement (e.g., if one party's actions depend on getting outside approval). [**See page 166.**]

> *Mr. White agrees to stop construction while Ms. Black seeks a home-improvement loan. Ms. Black agrees to notify Mr. White in writing by July 31 as to whether he should proceed. If Mr. White does not receive notification by that date, he may cancel their construction contract and keep her deposit.*

It won't be perfect

No agreement is a perfect or guaranteed fix. Help them set a positive direction as best you can.

Closing

**SUMMARY:
CLOSING**

---

1. **Read aloud and have everyone sign**

2. **Note what they have accomplished**

3. **Reconfirm what will be kept confidential**

4. **Take care of any logistics, fees, follow-up**

5. **Invite reflections**

Wish them well.

▶ Plan to end on time

Ending on time takes forethought. Aim to finish the work of the session with 15 minutes to spare. This gives you enough room for wrap-up, review, evaluations, and logistics.

As soon as you can see they aren't going to get through the whole Topic List in time to end on schedule, let them know, and recommend a follow-up session. If they prefer to "power through," negotiate a revised end time. But if they seem to be flagging, or want to work past the 3-hour mark, take a substantive, mind-clearing break. Otherwise, attention and goodwill may slip away.

▶ Purpose of a thought-out closing

Emotions can run high, even euphoric, at the end of a final session. Participants may feel relieved, wary, sad, excited, disappointed, and tired, all at once. The Closing is a time to acknowledge these feelings and to bring the mediation to a positive close. It allows for catching loose ends, having a ritual to confirm the agreement, transitioning to next steps, and taking a moment to reflect on how much they have accomplished together.

Closing

4.8
SOME THINGS YOU CAN APPRECIATE

- Their willingness to meet and speak frankly.

- Speaking from the heart.

- The energy and goodwill they have invested.

- Learning more about each other's situation.

- Clearing up misunderstandings.

- Reaching agreement.

1. Reading and signing

✓ If they've reached an agreement, read it aloud. People catch different things when they hear a text versus seeing it.

✓ Ask the parties to confirm their commitment by signing the document. You may choose to sign as a witness. [**But see page 71.**]

✓ Give each party a copy. The limelight and the credit is theirs at this moment, even if the mediators have worked hard.

2. Note what they have accomplished

✓ Compliment them on whatever deserves recognition. Don't overdo it; be brief and sincere.

3. Reconfirm what will be kept confidential

✓ Double-check that participants are in sync about what they've agreed to hold confidential, and what they will share with whom.

✓ Where appropriate, review what, if anything, the mediator will report to a supervisor, a referral source, the media, or other interested parties.

4. Logistics, fees, follow-up, reminders

✓ Review any follow-up the mediators have agreed to do.

✓ Underscore participants' plans for how to communicate with each other if problems come up in the future.

5. Invite reflections

If the mood seems right, ask for their reflections on the work they've done today. They may comment on the mediators or mediation process, or they may report how they feel—tired, satisfied, appreciative, relieved it's over.

Sometimes people open up significant conversation as the mediation is ending ("I've always wondered, why did X happen?"), or express regrets. If it seems like a meaningful moment between them, stay in the background and make space for it, even if the hour is late.

….Wish them well!!

4.9
REFLECTION QUESTIONS

- *How did the session go for you today?*

- *How are you feeling about the work you did today?*

- *Is there anything else you want to say to me or to each other?*

- *Any thoughts or suggestions about today you would like to mention?*

Afterwards: Wrapping up

SUMMARY:
WRAP-UP

1. Complete paperwork, note follow-up tasks

2. Keep essential information only, destroy notes

3. Note down your self-evaluation thoughts

4. Appreciate your own hard work, celebrate your successes

▶ Participant evaluation

You may want to ask evaluation questions during the "invite reflections" part of the Closing:

- **What was their reaction** to the mediation? To the way you mediated?

- **What have they have observed** or learned today?

It's a good practice to also have an evaluation form for them to fill out, and to routinely gather feedback to improve your mediation. See pages 184–86 for mediator self-evaluation and session evaluation. For links to evaluation templates go to **mediatorshandbook.com**.

▶ Mediator's self- and session evaluation

Write down problems, breakthroughs, or other observations that will be helpful to you and maybe to other mediators. Do it now! It's surprising how fast memory fades, especially if you mediate often.

Working with a co-mediator offers you a chance to get feedback from a knowledgeable colleague who has just watched you in action. Press yourself to be as receptive and as candid as you can. Future participants deserve good mediators!

Multiple sessions

▶ At the end of the current session

➤ Make sure they are actively willing to participate in a next session, not just going along with the idea to be polite.

➤ Write up any decisions they have already made, and give them each a copy to take home today—people sometimes change their minds later about participating in a follow-up session. (You can also email it—see below.)

➤ Review tasks each has agreed to do before the next session—get an appraisal, draw up a budget, consult a lawyer.

➤ Agree on how they will interact between sessions.

➤ Invite them to call you between sessions if any concerns arise.

▶ Between sessions

➤ Jot down your notes and facilitation plans right after the session, while your memory is fresh.

➤ Email the parties a summary of topics covered and any decisions reached at the previous session. Remind them what "homework" they agreed to do or actions they agreed to take, and what topics remain to be discussed.

➤ Again invite them to call you if any concerns arise. (If only one person calls, you need not call the other. Equal opportunity is enough.)

➤ Do not conduct Separate Conversations by email, and be very careful what you put in writing when responding to parties' emails.

▶ At the beginning of the next session

Conflicts constantly evolve, sometimes rapidly. Be ready for new topics, shifts in attitude, changes to the last session's decisions.

➤ Start with a go-round for each person to report on any progress, new information, or rethinking.

➤ Review previous decisions, what topics remain to be discussed, and how much of it you think they can cover today. If it seems likely that another session will be needed, and you haven't already mentioned this possibility, mention it now.

➤ **Confirm** their goals and remaining topics, adjust as needed.

UNDERSTANDING CONFLICT

THE TOOLBOX

5

Disputes & conflicts

"Why are they behaving like this? "What do they really want?" This chapter offers a few perspectives on conflict to help mediators assess what's going on and facilitate effectively. Some participants may also find these concepts helpful in understanding their conflict differently.

▶ Disputes: The flashpoint of conflict

The surface of life is full of annoyances, limited resources, dislikes, clashing needs, surging hormones, cultural divides, put-downs, opposing opinions, and irreconcilable interpretations. These are organic, an inevitable part of everyday human experience, not an aberration or an interruption.

Most of the time we negotiate our incompatible needs and perspectives as best we can, and keep going. "Disputes" are open disagreements about specific incidents and issues that have proved difficult to resolve or let go. They may arise from a one-time event, such as an accident. More often they are a visible flashpoint in an ongoing state of tension and distress we define as "conflict."

Disputes can potentially be reconfigured or resolved through decisions made by the parties or for them. Resolving underlying conflicts is more challenging: business partners can decide to share profits 50–50, but can't just decide to feel trusting toward each other.

Interpersonal disputes often expand into conflicts when:

- There's significant emotional investment because they believe something important is at stake.

- Commitment to the relationship is not strong enough to hang in there and try to communicate and problem-solve. Or there's no relationship to begin with (conflicts between strangers).

- People lack conflict-resolution skills (not IF they argue, but HOW).

- People lack the resources to create solutions that work.

- They need the other party's cooperation.

Conflicts aren't broken parts that can be fixed up as good as new, like replacing the transmission of a car. Parties may believe that if the other side just did X, all would be well, but this is usually wishful thinking. There are people, relationships, networks, and systems involved. Major conflicts — and their resolution — tend to leave marks. They change how people see themselves and feel about each other. They alter the trajectory of our lives.

Metaphors for understanding conflict

▶ Weather

Being in a conflict can be confusing—who is involved, what are their motives, who knows about this, what are the rules, what is this thing about anyway? In this way, conflict is like the weather, with its cycles of hot and cold, storms and sun, rain and ice, its unpredictable waves and winds. It forces you to pay attention. To disputing parties, interactions with the other party can feel similarly capricious and out of control. Episodes come and go, lightning bolts flash, the sun comes out for a while, and their emotions ride up and down.

Mediation will not leave them in a permanently sunny universe. Ultimately neither party is going to do exactly what the other wants, or be who they want them to be. Ideally, the parties leave mediation with the protection of a workable plan, and a willingness to communicate enough that they can live with the ebb and flow of the irreconcilable aspects of their differences.

▶ Game of chess

In reality, people do have some control of their conflict "weather." They make choices that influence what happens and how they feel about it. From this perspective, conflict is more like a chess game. People take turns making moves based on their guesses about how the other party will respond. They try to limit the other side's ability to do harm, and they shore up their own positions. A player can't go back and undo; they have to take their next step based on where the game has brought them. Unlike chess, however, each "player" operates from a different set of unspoken rules (cultural norms, expectations from previous experiences, social and legal rules, etc.).

The mediator becomes yet another player, also making moves and trying to predict how parties will respond to one facilitation approach or another. The mediator also becomes the game master, getting the parties to talk instead of make unilateral moves. This means checking out their assumptions about each other and discussing what the rules of the game should be—how do they interact with each other? How do they decide what a fair resolution is? The chess metaphor recognizes that people are not helpless in the face of conflict: they have made active choices before, and they can take action now.

Metaphors for understanding conflict

▶ All the world's a stage

Conflict as a story. Over time, as people recount their conflict experiences, a story emerges, one that tries to make sense of the information they have and the feelings they've experienced. The audience — oneself, family and friends, and later people with the power to intervene — also influences what gets put in, what gets left out, what meanings and emotions are attached. The more the story is repeated, the more people may identify with their role as victim, as hero, as conciliator, as innocent, as protector, as the reasonable one, and cast the other party in the opposing role.

Conflict as theater. Whenever people with different narratives interact, you get drama, complete with characters, episodes, themes, plots, moral lessons, and unexpected twists to the tale. Mediation itself is just one act of the play — who knows whether it will be the final scene?

Participants don't just tell their story, they perform it. In mediation, they seem to want the other side to match their own level of intensity. Quieter people may try to calm the other party down or withdraw till they do. Emotive people may push and goad until they receive a strong emotional response. Kindly people may express caring or make a concession, trying to get a respectful discussion going.

Mediators can't direct the play much, but they do create the setting and serve as an attentive audience. In the process, participants gradually revise their scripts to tell a richer story with more strands and nuances — a story that includes other people's perspectives and casts themselves as people who can construct their own future.

▶ Conflict as energy for change in a system

Conflict is a symptom of imperfect human systems — corporations, marriages, communities. Almost every aspect of a system causes difficulties for somebody. Rules and expectations don't fit. Information doesn't flow to the right places. People fight about who sets goals or makes decisions. Resources are distributed unevenly. People argue about boundaries or policies. All systems encourage some behaviors and forbid others, and benefit some at the expense of others. Conflict is an ever-present "adjustment mechanism." A human system is like an ecosystem, not a machine, so adjusting one part affects the rest. This is why you need all the right people and information in the room to come up with wise changes.

The conflict core

5.1
WHAT'S AT THE CORE?

Questions to ask yourself:

What is each person afraid of? What are they protecting?

How have they been hurt already?

What boundaries have been violated, what lines have been crossed?

What opportunities are they reaching for?

What sense of self are they defending?

What does this person care deeply about?

Who does this person care deeply about?

What does their "problem" symbolize or represent to them?

What metaphors and storylines do they use?

[See page 149.]

From the outside, a dispute can seem irrational, overblown, or just plain trivial. Why are people fighting about this small stuff? Why are they repeating themselves over and over? Why can't they have a civil conversation and figure this thing out?

It seems unlikely that people would repeatedly choose to expend their intense life energy like this unless a situation affects them — significantly. All conflicts, even the driest of business and legal disputes, are driven by issues of identity, fear, caring, self-worth, and power. Parties aren't just trying to settle tangible differences — to fix the problem. At another level they are struggling over whose version of reality will win out.

People become emotionally embroiled in a conflict when something important is threatened, when fighting for something helps establish who they are, who they love, what they stand for.

The questions in Sidebar 5.1 help a mediator find the participants' guiding motivations and interests, whether you ask them out loud or silently use them as guides for your own observations. These questions reflect a set of assumptions about what often motivates conflict behaviors:

➢ **At the core of conflict, people are protecting** themselves, the people they love, and those things they most care about (e.g., a project, a belief, a piece of property, an organization, their status, a source of income), even if their behavior doesn't seem loving or passionate from the outside.

➢ **Anger and fear, gain and loss.** In mediation, people are angry about harm that has been done to that core, or fearful about what might happen to it. Their actions try to prevent further losses or actively seek more power or resources to strengthen their interests. With its shadow of potential violence, the display of anger can be particularly difficult to deal with. On the positive side, it demonstrates a strong desire for change which, if acknowledged but contained, can propel parties into trying a new direction.

➢ **Hurt and distress add another layer** of self-protectiveness. When the actions of a once trusted person damage a relationship, or denigrate someone's self-image or public image, they may experience grief, fear, betrayal, violation, and intense anger. Acidic feelings about the other person, such as scorn or disgust, are hard to turn around. Even if wounded parties reach a mediated agreement on substantive issues, they may not be willing or able to piece a relationship back together. Mutual regret, deep listening, and efforts to make amends can all help, and sometimes on a good day, a turning point comes, and parties are unexpectedly able to appreciate and care about each other again.

The conflict core

Who do they love?

What are they seeking?

What are they protecting?

We won't be able to afford it anymore.

This is humiliating.

We've been shut out.

If they get away with this, they'll take advantage of us again and again.

Their lies could ruin my good reputation.

They are making decisions without consulting us.

I might lose my kids.

HURT

Our people deserve respect.

We might be attacked again.

LOVE

She thinks I'm stupid.

I might get fired.

DESIRE

They betrayed me. I'll never trust them again.

ATTACHMENT

We can't pay our bills.

My kids could get hurt.

FEAR

No one will listen to me after this.

This will bankrupt us.

I hate feeling intimidated.

I won't be the expert any longer.

He might kill me.

I need my privacy.

I won't belong any more.

I'm losing influence.

What are they afraid of?

What might they lose?

What is the hurt?

Common effects of conflict

Conflict is not just a set of problems and differences — it's an emotional and social *experience*. Becoming absorbed in a conflict can affect a person's mind, their wallet, their body, their heart, their relationships, and their sense of self. The following are just a few of the effects of conflict that can make mediation challenging.

HANDLING ANGER, ANXIETY, STRESS	• **Avoiding** the other parties, not acknowledging the conflict. • **Turning it inward.** Sleeplessness, illness, guilt, embarrassment, shame, depression, envy, fear, defensiveness, addiction. • **Directing it outward.** Making accusations, blaming and feeling victimized, attacking (physically or verbally), suspicion, revenge, gathering allies, calling in authorities. • **Reverting to familiar patterns.** People try harder rather than smarter, sticking with their tried and true ways of doing or thinking about things.
EFFECT ON PERCEPTIONS	• **Narrow, rigid notions** about "the problem," the facts, and acceptable solutions. • **Brain freeze.** Difficulty taking in information that contradicts one's feelings or interpretations. Difficulty thinking logically or imaginatively. • **Hyper-focus** of attention and feelings, sharpening some areas of thinking and memory, while distorting others. • **Seeing one's own actions as a response to circumstances.** • **Seeing the other party's actions as self-serving,** deliberate attacks by a person who is *by nature* mean, stupid, greedy, immoral, evil, or crazy. • **Adversarial mindset.** Self-protective and self-absorbed. Seeing the situation as a zero-sum game: if they win, I lose.
RELATIONS WITH THE OTHER PARTY	• **Interactions become tense and less frequent or happen indirectly** through other people. • **Instead of talking, people take action.** Instead of discussing, they watch and infer. Those actions become fraught with meaning and interpretation. • **The goals of punishing** the other side and protecting oneself may become more important than getting what they originally wanted. Demands and retaliation become harsher, compromise unacceptable. • **Identity lines are drawn more sharply,** as are allegiances. Disputes flare up around identity symbols (clothing, colors, ownership of land, language choice, etc.).

The pleasures of conflict

OK, we need to be honest. For some people, conflict is the reason they get out of bed in the morning. Being in a fight can be satisfying, even exciting. Conflict is a way to gain resources and social status, to feel honorable and strong, to take pleasure in one's power. Conflict can create camaraderie and a stronger sense of community and identity. It's a mental challenge too, an opportunity to learn.

As they come closer to an agreement, parties may realize (consciously or not) that they will have to let go of some of these satisfactions. When you sense push-back during the mediation, ask yourself:

What satisfactions are they giving up?

- Enjoying the intrigue: investigating, strategizing, surprising.

- Thinking deeply about important issues.

- Getting revenge, getting even. Hurting people who have hurt them.

- The sheer physical pleasure of venting, the catharsis that comes after expressing strong emotion.

- Feeling a strong sense of identity and loyalty.

- The satisfaction of standing up for themselves.

- Gaining allies, buddies, or a sympathetic audience.

- Fighting for something important.

- Feeding on the drama—the intensity of emotion, the ability to make the other side react, the fun of giving flavorful updates to their friends.

- Breaking rules they don't like. Annoying people they don't like.

- Knowing they are right. Feeling righteous, superior.

- Being part of a larger movement, a just cause.

- Getting a lot of attention that makes them feel important.

- Taking on authorities.

- Feeling powerful.

- Winning!! Feeling vindicated, getting what they want.

Such color and drama! Such sense of purpose! Such attention! In comparison, the mediation conversation may seem pallid, a tedious and compromising letdown. Can mediators help them find some excitement and pleasure in reconnecting, solving a knotty problem, creating something new, or doing the right thing?

When things heat up

The previous two pages on the negative and pleasurable effects of conflict show how much turmoil people may be experiencing—often on several levels at once. Small wonder that disputing parties often feel discouraged by the time they get to mediation! Even disputes that appear relatively straightforward are a tangle of relationships, memories, events, beliefs, perceptions. It reminds mediators to stay humble: There's lots more going on than the participants will talk about, and much you will never know or understand.

▶ Conflict Spiral

When it gets personal

Mediation is well-suited to resolving disputes about substance—when people have conflicting interests and goals, or can't agree on HOW to reach mutual goals. Once their different perceptions, information, and emotions are on the table, parties can generally make practical decisions.

As conflict escalates, the parties' main aim turns personal—wanting to punish each other and win the battle (or at least not lose it). Mediation becomes more difficult—but also potentially more valuable. It may take a while to downshift the level of anger and fear enough to restart communication and to understand each other's distress and hopes.

When it gets political

As conflict intensifies, its ripples may affect more people, more tasks, and more decisions. Alliances and splits may form among friends and colleagues, then spread to whole organizations or communities.

Parties may get help from appealing to others, but will also lose some control over their conflict. When an outside authority intervenes, or the dispute "goes public," others start defining what the conflict is about and how it should be dealt with. (Mediation is unusual in that it gives the parties back the power to define and resolve their conflict—if they choose to take it.)

Eventually, a conflict may coalesce around issues of ideology or identity that divide one group from another. Representatives speak on behalf of groups, with advisors and experts assisting. At this point, an interpersonal dispute becomes just one of many within a larger conflict, and resolving it may not get much attention—or even be possible. Resolving these larger conflicts requires additional methods and knowledge that are beyond the scope of this handbook.

The way out is through

When people have an overt and emotional conflict, they may hope to end the discomfort by coming to a quick compromise. But unless they discuss the dynamics of the situation and the underlying interests, similar problems are likely to surface again. To converge on a more durable resolution, parties first need to go through the hard work of openly disagreeing with each other. Viewpoints will diverge. Emotions will get out of hand. Solutions may seem impossible.

In their superb book, *A Facilitator's Guide to Participatory Decision-Making*, Sam Kaner and his coauthors dub this phase "the Groan Zone." The message is: spending time hashing things out is unavoidable. It feels bad. People can get through it. Somehow labeling their experience as "being in the Groan Zone" seems to lighten things up for people and offer them a bit of hope.

The agreement is only a piece of the outcome. It's the act of sitting down, face to face, and working *through* their concerns, understanding the various consequences—intended or unintended, immediate and longer term—that pushes the door open to reconciliation and workable changes.

▶ Focusing on the concrete details

"Working it through" means getting into the weeds, talking about details. Conflict often expresses itself in disputes about concrete things—objects, actions, rules, behaviors, events. Likewise, in mediation, exploring participants' disagreements through tangible examples of behaviors and their impact gives people a vehicle to discuss their relationship and their emotions. Two roommates can talk about how angry they feel, how the friendship isn't working—but it is hard to know where to go with this after a while. If, on the other hand, they talk about the dirty laundry, about how often the boyfriend stays overnight, or rules for borrowing the car, these are an indirect way of discussing "how do we interact?" "How much do we care for each other?" "Is there a future in this relationship, and if so, what should it look like?"

For this reason, our mediation model keeps bringing people back to specific descriptions—of behavior, impacts, systems that don't work, topics that need decisions, options—not because problem-solving is the only goal, but because it's in talking about the dispute's *details* that interests and feelings and connections become clear. Changing something concrete impacts people's lives, and also changes their feelings and relationship in the longer term. In this way, specific agreements give emerging shoots of reconciliation a place to take root.

The Conflict Triangle

PEOPLE

**Who is fighting and
how are they experiencing it?**

- Personalities, mood

- Emotions, hurts, longings

- Empathy, affection

- Values, interpretations

- Behaviors, skills, abilities

- Identities

- Perceptions of self, other

- Patterns of interaction

- Relative social status

- Relationship roles & history, degree
  of intimacy

PROCESS

How are they fighting?

- How people communicate

- How discussions go

- How information is handled

- Who is included, excluded

- Structures, systems

- Procedures, laws, rules, & enforcement

- Authority, roles

- Division of responsibilities

- Norms about how to behave in a
  conflict

- How decisions are made

PROBLEM

What are they fighting about?

- Disagreements

- Concerns, worries

- Blame, accusation

- Explanations and reasons

- Positions, proposed solutions

- Fallouts from past

- Information, data, facts

- Interests, needs, wants

- Interdependence of parties

- Limits, systems, laws, rules

- Subject-matter specifics, technicalities

- Perceived options and consequences

People, Process, Problem

▶ The Conflict Triangle

Each conflict has its own context: who the people are, how they are interacting, what problems they want to solve—"people, process, and problem" for short. We refer to this context as the "Conflict Triangle."

➤ **People: WHO is fighting and how are they connected?** Parties have particular personalities, emotions, and relationships. The conflict has a particular history, set in a particular social context.

➤ **Process: HOW are they fighting?** Parties do things that intensify, ease, spread, or defuse a conflict. Their interactions are shaped by their environment—rules, hierarchy, decision-making modes, laws, norms for communication, etc.—or by taking part in a mediation.

➤ **Problem: WHAT are they fighting about and why?** Parties have particular concerns, needs, values that ignite or drive the dispute.

Mediators must attend to all three aspects throughout the process, as a lasting resolution must account for all three sides of the conflict triangle.

▶ 3 sets of tools for the mediator's toolbox

For mediators, each side of the triangle requires a somewhat different mindset and skills. The next three "Toolbox" chapters look at each in turn:

- Supporting the People
- Facilitating the Process
- Solving the Problem

Each chapter reviews skills and concepts, laying out details and examples that expand on the instructions in the three earlier chapters on "getting to the table" and the mediation session. The Toolbox is intended as a resource for ongoing learning and reference—don't feel you have to take in everything at once!

Start by noticing which People/Process/Problem mode you tend towards when you participate in meetings or mediations. Is your first instinct to connect with people? To redirect the conversation? Or to focus on tasks and information? See examples on the next page of how a mediator might respond to arguing parties using each mode.

The goal is to become fluent in all three modes, so that you have more tools at hand. Since none of us ever achieves complete balance, look for co-mediators whose strengths can complement yours.

Which mode are you in?

The parties are standing up and yelling at each other. Here is how a mediator might respond in each mode.

SUPPORT MODE

This has been upsetting for everyone involved, hasn't it? [Empathy]

It's really obvious that you all care passionately about this organization [common goal], *and you're feeling angry and stuck* [Acknowledge feelings].

You've both said you intend to keep your jobs [personal goals]. *Pause.* [Use silence.]

From what you've said so far, I think you can find a way to work through these disagreements [encouragement]. *What would make it easier for you to talk with each other?* [Discuss interaction, relationship.]

First, let's take a break for a few minutes. [Attend to physical needs.]

PROCESS MODE

Let's pause here for a moment [Interrupt unproductive escalation], *and check where you want to go with this.* [Consult.]

I'd like to change gears here for a moment, and talk about topic X before we come back to this harder issue again. [Change subject/direction.]

From what I hear, the three things you most disagree about are A, B, and C, is that right? [Summarize, check.]

I'm a bit confused about the sequence of events you're talking about. Can you sketch out a time-line here on the board? [Take a new direction, use visuals, get them working on a joint task.]

You keep slipping into heated arguments—is that okay with you, or would you like to change how or what you're talking about? [Check in about process.]

Let's take a half hour break, and the mediators will touch base with each of you. [Use Separate Conversations, change the pace and approach.]

PROBLEM-SOLVING MODE

Phew, this really is a hot issue, isn't it? [Focus on content.]

Help me sort this out here—can you each give me ONE example of something the other person did or said that upset you, and what impact that had on you? [Ask for examples of behavior + impact.]

It sounds like what matters most to each of you is X and Y. [Focus on their interests.]

You each have different information about this incident… Let's review what each of you know. [Fill in information gaps, check interpretations.]

What do you need to know in order to make good decisions about reallocating job responsibilities? [Future focus, topic focus.]

SUPPORTING THE PEOPLE

THE TOOLBOX

6

Supporting the people: Main skills

▶ Partial to all

"Supporting" approaches help people say what they need to say, hear the other parties, and begin cooperating with each other.

As mediator, you need a certain detachment to avoid "playing favorites." It keeps you from being pulled in or pulling away, from slipping into advocating for the weaker or nicer party. At the same time, each participant needs the mediators' active, positive support. "Impartial" doesn't mean "indifferent"! Perhaps it's better to think of being *equally partial* towards every person, to honor each point of view, to give your full attention and empathy to all.

▶ Key points

➤ **Listen carefully and with sympathetic interest.** Then reflect back, acknowledging their views, needs, and feelings. This is probably THE most important thing you can do.

➤ **Never make them "wrong."**

➤ **Be patient, unhurried, accepting.** Participants may not be organized or thinking clearly. Be tender with their frustration, confusion, and anxiety.

➤ **Respect, but don't press for, emotions.** Reflect back the emotions you sense, being careful not to guess or project your own. Beyond that, follow their lead as to how vulnerable or revealing they choose to be. When they express strong feelings, watch how the others react; if they seem to be okay with it, step back and let things unfold.

➤ **Prevent hostile exchanges.** If they are sliding into attack and counterattack, intervene right away. To avoid escalation, get them to *describe* the impact of the conflict, so that they don't need to *display* their distress about it. Keep them talking about themselves — their experiences and needs — rather than about the other party.

➤ **Don't try to persuade them of ANYTHING** — of how to behave, of what "makes sense" — though you do want to ask questions that help them think through an issue. It helps to face the speaker when you reflect back — e.g., restate to Brian what you heard him say, rather than explaining to Dora what Brian said.

6.1
SHOWING EMPATHY

- *I can see you're both under a lot of stress.*

- *That must have been a painful choice to make.*

- *This situation would be tough for anybody.*

- *Sounds like you're very sad about the way it turned out.*

- *It's been a rough time for everyone here.*

- *So, that really upset you.*

- *Work relationships can be very hard — you didn't choose to work together, but here you are together 5, 6 hours a day.*

- *Uh-huhs, nods, etc., that show you are following (though not agreeing or disagreeing).*

Setting the tone

▶ Tone

"Tone" encompasses the attitudes, feelings, and expectations you project through your demeanor and voice. To illustrate how much this matters, try reading aloud any example of "what the mediator says" in this book, and notice how a slight change in inflection or body language can make it sound friendly, commanding, interested, no-nonsense, condescending, irritated, or sympathetic.

Like taxi drivers who watch their passenger's reactions and fine-tune their conversation accordingly, mediators can vary their tone, pace, and style to help parties settle down and to give them encouragement. For example, parties to a business dispute may appreciate a crisp tone that suggests efficiency and structure, while people suffering emotional pain may respond to a slower pace, and a tone of compassion and hope.

➤ **Project concern, confidence, curiosity.** Parties seem to respond well when the mediator's stance is one of concern, relaxed confidence, and gentle curiosity.

➤ **Convey a sense of "This is normal, this is getting somewhere"** (if it is true!). Be a calm presence amid the storm—you've been here before and seen things work out.

➤ **Adjust the pace and volume:** down if they are having arguments, or up if the conversation stagnates. Lively or efficient conversation is okay as long as everyone can keep up. Quieter moments can turn the mediation around. After something painful or kind is said, hold the silence a good bit longer than you would in everyday conversations.

▶ Be yourself

➤ **Set the tone in a low-profile way** that doesn't put your personality and performance center-stage.

➤ **Be yourself.** It takes less of your attention, and comes across as real. Anyway, there's probably more than enough posturing going on at the table already. If you are naturally clipped and practical, or you are generally warm and humorous, stay that way, tuning it up or down depending on how they seem to respond.

➤ **Ultimately it's about your mindset**, not external performance. Your inner stance will be revealed through your face, body, and voice—probably more than you realize—so you may have to consciously adjust your thoughts or attitude in order to change your tone.

Level of formality, taking notes

▶ Everyday language

Using everyday conversational language can help everyone follow the discussion and set an egalitarian tone.

➤ **Use a conversational style during the Opening**, and be cautious throughout about using specialized mediation terms.

➤ **Watch for phrases which might be seen as talking down to the participants.** "I'd like you to…," "I need you to…." (They aren't there to satisfy you.) "Please wait your turn." (You want them to choose, not to obey.) Also avoid using the inclusive "we" when you actually mean "all of you" or "I."

➤ **Let participants speak in the natural flow of their own language** and style. They can become frustrated if the mediators try to get them to speak differently. If you paraphrase, always ask them if you got it right. Whether their style involves crude swearing or stiffly formal professionalese, suppress your biases about how people "should" speak and concentrate on the person's message.

▶ How formal?

Names. Even if the parties address each other as "Dean Richman" and "Nancy," use the same level of formality with both (Dean Richman and Ms. Green).

Culturally appropriate formality. Be alert for the parties' unspoken expectations about the formality of the mediator's language — folksy? professional? friendly? educated? plain-spoken? dignified? Take your cue from them. When there are power differences, showing you are both impartial AND respectful can be a culturally sticky challenge — get advice. [**See page 109.**]

▶ Taking notes

Explain you are taking notes only to help you keep track — letting them know you'll destroy them at the end of the mediation. Keep an eye out for their reactions. They may see note-taking as giving careful attention, or conversely as not really listening. If you write copiously only when one person speaks, they may assume you're finding more of value — or conversely, finding more problems — with what that person is saying. Of course, using a flip chart resolves these questions by making your notes public.

Confidentiality in practice

In most conflicts, people are reluctant to reveal certain information and feelings, yet cannot reach a resolution until they do so. Inquire before the mediation whether confidentiality is a concern. Mediators can't ever promise that parties will keep confidentiality, but can help them reach an understanding about what they are willing to keep confidential from whom — and put it in writing if they want to.

▶ What you will keep confidential

Before the session, and again during Opening and Closing phases, confirm and adjust with the parties what you will hold confidential and with whom.

✓ **Information a party gives you privately**, what they say to you, any documents they give you, their contact information.

✓ **Information provided during a session**, anything anyone, including you, says at the table, any documents or other written information the parties provide, any documents you create or notes you take during the session.

✓ **The fact that a mediation occurred**, what happened in the sessions, what the outcome was, and the terms of any agreement.

✓ **Your opinions of the people involved**, of what was discussed, of the fact that there's a dispute, or of the dispute's subject matter.

From whom?

✓ **Check what information the parties consider public.** In a high-profile dispute, discuss what information you can give to the media.

✓ **Ask what you can report** to the referral source, supervisors, or other interested nonparticipants.

✓ **Tell them what records you will keep**, who has access to them.

Exceptions

Tell them at the start what you will report to others. This may include:

✓ **Any threat to harm** other **participants**, or those close to them.

✓ **Any harm** you think the parties' private agreement might do to others outside the mediation (organization, company, community).

✓ **Information you are professionally obligated to report** (e.g., as a teacher or social worker), such as suspected child abuse.

Giving your full attention

▶ Why giving full attention is essential

Every mediation skill rests on being genuinely "present" to the people around the table. Giving full attention means listening and observing with your mind, your heart, and your intuition. It means absorbing what the person is communicating, rather than planning your response.

➤ **Listen to create connection.** Being attentive is the starting point for respect and trust. It creates a connection between you and the participants, between you and their stories, between their past and their future.

➤ **Listen to understand their world.** Mediators attend to many layers of information at once:

- Facts about the substance of the dispute.

- Participants' perceptions, interpretations, and emotional states.

- Their interests, needs, desires, values, priorities.

- How they are interacting with each other and with you.

➤ **Listen to create an impartial yet caring, non-judgmental space.** It's an art to listen without seeming to agree or wanting to persuade.

➤ **Listen so they will move towards cooperation.** Talking to an attentive listener helps people to release emotions, unload what's on their mind, and get a clearer sense, themselves, about what they think and feel.

▶ Notice your own reactions and intuition

➤ **Did your attention drift?** Notice what distracted you or made it hard to listen. Remind yourself why you want to listen. Ask them to repeat what they said.

➤ **Catch your biases.** Monitor your physical reactions and thoughts. This can help you be more aware of your own "hot buttons," things that can make you favor one side, pull you off-center.

➤ **Listen to your intuition.** Your internal voice and gut feelings can help you understand the participants and their situation, especially what's not being said, and emotions that haven't quite surfaced.

Elements of full attention

- Set your inner dial and your outer body language to "receiving."

- Take in the emotions as well as the content the speaker is conveying.

- "Soften" your focus to be aware of their interactions with others, the wider context, the subtexts, the reactions of others who are listening.

- Accept that they are giving you THEIR truth. Even lies and delusions arise from something that is true within their inner landscape.

- Assume that they see their actions and intent as justified, and that if you fully understood their circumstances, you might think so too.

- Try not to show your negative reactions to what they are saying (watch your tone, body language, pointed questions).

- Put aside thoughts of whether you approve, what *you* would have done, how they might fix the situation.

Receptive **Without Judgment**

Impartial **Caring**

- Occasionally look towards the other participants, as well as at the speaker.

- Take care that your nods, "uh-huhs," or body language don't make you appear to be siding with the speaker. Give full attention but with some degree of detachment.

- Be warm and "partial" towards all, rather than sympathetic towards none. Impartiality doesn't mean indifference.

- (If these points seem contradictory, yes, merging empathic listening with impartiality is a tension inherent in the mediator role.)

- Find out what is meaningful and true for this person.

- See the speaker as a unique and valuable person—albeit a person who may not be at their best today.

- Acknowledge the pain the person has experienced in living with this conflict.

- Find something good about an unpleasant person that helps you want the best for them.

Acknowledging

"Acknowledging" means showing you've understood the essence of what a person has experienced, what they want, and how they feel, without judging them or the situation. (It's like "reflecting back" and other re-wording tools [**see page 128**], but with a focus on conveying empathy.)

Acknowledging puts people at ease—helps them calm down, think more clearly, soften their adversarial stance. Being acknowledged in the presence of an adversary can sometimes go farther toward resolving a conflict than problem-solving does!

Important: When you acknowledge, do it facing them; don't explain their view to the other party.

Acknowledge their experiences and interests

Repeat or paraphrase what they said, or summarize their key point(s), without injecting your opinion. Don't "tell" them what they said—use a questioning tone or ask a question to invite confirmation or correction. If you repeat a judgmental remark, add, "from your point of view…"

> *After the argument you guys had last February, he started arriving late to work and leaving early most days?*

> *They didn't tell you they were filing for bankruptcy, and from your point of view this was really irresponsible?*

> *It sounds like for you, Miriam, the important thing is keeping the street quiet and safe? And Dominic, you want to ensure customer parking is convenient to your theater?*

If you can't keep track. Take notes—or tactfully ask them to slow down, or repeat, or pause for you to summarize what you've heard so far. Or repeat back what you remember, and ask what you missed.

Acknowledge their feelings

Include their feelings in your paraphrase or summary. If they say how they feel (angry, fed up), use their words; if they don't, take a cue from their voice and face—or from what you might feel in their shoes.

Rather than "put on" a sympathetic tone, if you can briefly experience the same feeling in your body (true empathy), your tone and face will instinctively show more convincing signs that you "get it":

> *So his cancelling that meeting was the last straw for you?*

> *You were not only angry at being ignored–you got worried you'd flub the project if you were kept out of the loop?*

> *After he died, and she didn't call to see how you were doing, that made you even sadder, eh?*

**6.2
AN OPPORTUNITY
FOR *THEM* TO
ACKNOWLEDGE**

Late in the mediation, and only if the moment is right, you might give the parties an opening to acknowledge each other. Be sure not to put anyone on the spot, should they have nothing nice to say.

- *It sounds like you feel some regret…*

- *If you could do it over again, is there anything you might have done differently?*

- *You have a chance to clear the slate today—any thanks or appreciations, any apologies or regrets you might want to bring up?*

- *It seems like you both have things you respect about each other…?*

THE TOOLBOX
Supporting the People

Handling judgmental remarks

When they are judging each other, redirect the conversation to the two basics: examples of behavior and its impact. If they get caught in an attack-defend cycle, interrupt and defuse or ask questions that redirect them back to sharing information.

JUDGMENTS ABOUT:	POSSIBLE APPROACHES	WHAT THE MEDIATOR MIGHT SAY
Values or principles "A good mother would discipline her children when they get out of line."	Connect the judgment to a truth or principle both sides will probably agree with. Or ignore the judgment and respond to the information contained in it. Ask what behavior the speaker finds problematic. Check out assumptions.	*Figuring out how to teach kids discipline is important. It seems like different parents have a lot of different approaches to it.* *You absolutely don't want Marge to leave it up to the kids whether they climb your fence.* *You're wondering if Marge talked to her kids about not climbing the fence?* [To Marge:] *Do you want to respond?*
Character "Morris is reckless and clumsy, truly a danger to the work team."	Reflect back the emotion and content, leaving the judgments out. Ask what behavior and impacts led to that characterization.	*You worry about safety and liability in working with Morris.* *Can you give us an example of how Morris works that makes you uneasy?*
Behavior "You McBickers are always complaining about something!"	Ask what behavior they would find helpful next time. Avoid arguments about how to characterize previous behaviors ("complaining" or "mean").	*If a problem comes up for the McBickers, how would you like them to let you know about it?*
Needs and feelings "No one's discriminating against you. It's all in your head." "You don't need a car, you just want one to look cool."	Note that people can have different perceptions, then go back to examples of what people actually did and said. Ask the speaker what the impact on them would be if the other person's wish was granted.	*Let's look at what happened that time—how you each experienced it.* *What problems are you thinking her having a car would cause?*

Protecting

The mediator is ethically responsible for taking steps to protect the parties from physical and psychological abuse, during mediation sessions or as an aftermath.

▶ Safety = prepare ahead

➤ **Screening.** Before deciding to mediate, ask each privately if there's any history of threats, abuse, or weapons. You may need to converse with a person a while about other things before they are willing to tell you.

➤ **Do not mediate situations if you suspect abuse has occurred(!)** unless you are specially trained in victim-offender mediation. What happens in mediation can trigger abuse afterwards.

➤ **Work with a co-mediator.**

➤ **Set the limits they want.** Participants at risk often know better what limits are needed to protect themselves. Ask them, and follow their lead.

➤ **Location.** Meet in a building with several exits and parking areas, and where there are other people around. A serene and orderly environment and a private break-out space are also helpful.

➤ **Strategic seating.** Place a table between volatile participants, seat them at a distance, or use soft upholstered chairs.

▶ At the table

Physical fights seem to be rare to non-existent in formal mediations, but threats and verbal attacks are routine.

➤ **Keep a close eye on the emotional temperature** of the discussion. Be ready to change topics, tone, or approach.

➤ **Step in** immediately to stop verbal attacks. Keep your cool; don't seem upset by it. [**See pages 134–35.**]

➤ **Ensure privacy.** Deflect prying questions or off-limits topics.

➤ **Use Separate Conversations.** Trust the person's judgment about what measures or risks they wish to take, and how you can help.

➤ **End the session if you're uneasy — don't give the real reason.** *I think we've gone as far as we can tonight.* You can have the parties leave at different times, escort someone to their car, or privately give them contact information for protective services. [**See pages 136–37.**]

From adversarial mode to cooperative mode

6.3
SHIFTING TO COOPERATIVE MODE

Validations

• *Can you share with us one value that is core to how you choose to parent?* [Opening warm-up.]

• *What's one thing your department has done this past year that you are proud of?* [Opening warm-up.]

• *You care a lot about this club, and have worked hard to attract many new members.* [Reflecting back with affirmations.]

Speaking to their best self

• *Let's think about this option from each person's perspective. What do you think will work for them as well as for yourself?*

• *I know you take your representative role here seriously, that lots of people are counting on you.*

▶ Signs of defensiveness

Adversarial behavior comes in several guises. Some people shield themselves, others go on the offensive. Because adversarial mode tends to lessen people's ability to think clearly or empathize, watch for what seems to trigger it.

➤ **Self-protection.** Defensive arguments are self-protective, often rooted in fear of losing face, or of taking blame.

➤ **Listen for these tones**: righteous indignation, sniping and sarcasm, stubbornness, tense and cautious responses, or complaining.

➤ **Name-calling or swearing.** People may resort to personal attacks if they fear they are losing. (They can't think of counter-arguments, or the other side isn't budging, or they feel they're getting a raw deal.)

▶ The mind shift

The goal is a shift in their thinking mode:

> *"He is a bad person."* ➡ *"His behavior is creating problems."*

> *"I have to protect myself."* ➡ *"We can figure this out."*

Mostly, it is the gradual sharing of information and interests that relaxes parties enough to move them in this direction. The next pages describe several facilitation approaches that can also help ease the parties' adversarial stance.

▶ Speak to their best self

You can't directly persuade people into cooperative mode. Even the mediator's respectful listening only gets so far. Most people cannot take in other perspectives until they feel that their own story has been heard, and that their own needs and grievances have been recognized.

➤ **Start with validation.** Look for opportunities to ask them about what they value, about something they do well. Self-affirmation helps people get into a less defensive frame of mind, and take in views and information that contradict their own.

➤ **Speak to their best self.** Visualize and speak to each person's best self. Nearly everyone has the ability to be principled, caring, and mature, when they aren't feeling ashamed or attacked. They may rise to your expectations.

From adversarial mode to cooperative mode

▶ Your mantra: Focus on their interests

When they are on the defensive or the attack, when they lose control, or dig in their heels — whatever the behavior — the mediator's mantra is always "speak to their interests." Participants in distress rarely care what you or the other parties want. If you want them to do something different, they have to see how it might help them meet their own needs.

> **Explore what frustrates them and what they hope for,** rather than examining how they feel or how they express that emotion.

> **Or step back and talk about communication.** What might make the discussion more useful and less stressful for them?

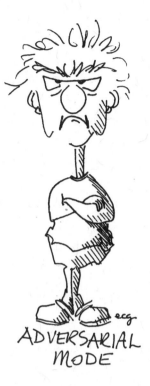

ADVERSARIAL
MODE

▶ Foster internal doubts.

As people begin to take in more of what others are saying, their armor of beliefs about the conflict may start to crack. The mediator can help them become more flexible by asking questions that separate facts from assumptions and misinformation, and by reality-testing their positions. Don't "tell" them, though — let them discover contradictions and take in the new information on their own.

▶ Don't make them wrong

> **Think about how you can alter the dynamic** between parties without implying that they are saying or doing something wrong:

> > *That's a valuable point you are making, and we WILL get there.*

> > *Can we back up a minute and make sure Edwin also responds before we go on?* (Not, "We're getting off topic.")

> **Find the place in yourself that knows** the discomfort of defensiveness and worry; talk to them from this place of empathy.

> **Help them save face** by calling their attention to your own confusion or fault. Find something (anything!) you don't understand — or apologize for some mistake or other. [**See page 135.**]

> > *I'm confused… I thought you were saying X, but now I see you meant…*

> > *I'm feeling a bit scattered here, sorry. Let me see if I can summarize where we are now.*

COOPERATIVE
MODE

Avoid this Kettle of Fish

Attending to comfort & accessibility

▶ Physical and energy needs

The mediator is also the host, responsible for everyone's comfort. Caring for people honors their efforts and helps set a warm, cooperative tone. When people are tired, thirsty, or irritable, it's hard for them to be fully present in the conversation.

➤ **Check-ins, breaks.** Don't get so lost in the subject matter that you forget to check in about their comfort! Try to have enough breaks that they don't have to request one. [**See page 53.**]

➤ **Provide water, also a light snack and other beverages** if possible. People are often too upset to feel like eating, but the gesture makes them feel better.

➤ **Control room temperature.** Check *beforehand*. Temperature directly affects mood and the ability to sustain attention.

▶ Accessibility needs

People may not tell you about health or accessibility issues. Inquire ahead of time, and keep alert to clues. Accessibility issues include:

➤ **Endurance.** For physical or mental reasons, some people may need shorter sessions, frequent breaks, or a better time of day.

➤ **Mobility and access:** Transit to/from the site, getting around the building, useable restrooms. Make sure everyone sits at eye-level to each other.

➤ **Attention challenges.** Do they need a calm environment, the ability to move around or stand, extra time to read or take in information?

➤ **Visual impairment.** Ask how the participant wants you to present written materials. Give them verbal information about visual cues from other participants. And good lighting helps everyone.

➤ **Reading.** Don't assume everyone can read quickly. Routinely summarize written materials and read the final agreement out loud.

➤ **Stress reactions.** If someone shows acute distress—an anxiety attack, splitting headache, complete loss of energy, explosive anger—take a break. Rushing to take care of one participant unasked can throw the balance off. Instead, at the table or in Separate Conversations, ask *all* parties if there's any way you can make them more comfortable.

Language and hearing difficulties

Participants with partial hearing loss, those who are deaf, and those who do not speak the other parties' language well face different challenges, but mediator accommodations for each are similar.

> **Ask** before the mediation about any hearing or language challenges. Participants may not bring it up themselves.

> **Most important**: Remind yourself that when someone has difficulty speaking fluently or understanding what's said, this does not reflect their ability to think clearly or to make considered decisions.

Structuring the process

> **Allow extra time** for each phase of the mediation, and take more frequent breaks. It can be hard to concentrate for long periods. Use this time to check in, to let parties confer in their own language.

> **Use visuals**, such as drawings, diagrams, and lists, preferably on a board or chart. Give everyone printouts of notes and agreement drafts — *only* if there's no problem with those papers leaving the mediation room.

> **Watch** how well the person is following the discussion, and whether other participants understand what the person is saying.

Communicating with the person

> **Face the person, speak naturally**, make sure they can see your mouth. For second-language speakers, make a small pause every sentence or two. For those hard of hearing, signal who the next speaker will be so they can watch from the start.

> **Reflect back and summarize often**, especially when others forget to accommodate during the heat of conversation.

> **Be relaxed and respectful** about the extra time and effort required of everyone present.

Working with interpreters

If possible, hire a professional interpreter. Otherwise locate a bilingual person who is not their friend or relative. Unskilled interpreters will convey what's happening selectively, and can too easily become *de facto* decision-makers. Talk ahead of time with the interpreter and the participant about how you will work together. Ask the interpreter to convey the non-verbal aspects of affect and tone, to explain cultural meanings, and to take extra care not to edit or advise.

Working with people in all their variety

▶ Identity

Identity is often a hot issue in mediation. It shapes how people present themselves, how they want to be seen and treated, who they "belong" to, and fundamentally how they think of themselves.

➤ **Foregrounding a particular identity.** We all have many identities to choose from (generation, race, religion, community, work and education, affiliations, gender—just for a start). Note which of these divide the parties, which ones they hold in common, which ones they embrace, which ones they overlook or actively hide.

➤ **Empowerment.** People identify with a group partly to make themselves more powerful—as a member, they may be able to claim respect, protection, allies, and resources.

➤ **Self-definition.** Parties may have a strong interest in honoring or asserting control over their public identities—for their own pride and sense of self, for the social and emotional bonds they have, and for economic or political benefits.

➤ **Dominance.** Parties may display their identity and status as a way to threaten or to get respect. Sometimes one party asserts power by imposing an unwelcome identity on the other—for example, by categorizing them ("You young people…") or invoking a stereotype.

➤ **Common identity** can motivate people to see each other as human beings, worthy of accommodation. *As parents, everyone here wants better quality schools.* Or, *How can you support each other as single women in your immigrant community?*

▶ Culture

Besides identity, many cultural influences affect a mediation session, especially ideas about why and how people should fight, how they should converse, and how they reach agreements.

Give yourself extra time for preparation and for listening when you are mediating culturally divergent groups. (These could be people from different professions or another part of the city, not just people of different races/ethnicity/nationality. Often it is the ones who look and talk like you that catch you by surprise.) Try to work with a culturally knowledgeable co-mediator or advisor. Observe, slow down, catch your assumptions. [**See examples at mediatorshandbook.com.**]

Finding commonalities

People in conflict usually have much more in common than they have differences, if only because being in proximity creates more opportunities for conflict. Yet the desire to differentiate themselves from "those people over there" means they often don't see their similarities.

Discover and remind them of what they have in common, especially during the first phase of mediation when people may see only their differences. *You all seem to think highly of Manuel… It sounds like you all want to find a way to make peace.*

If you have trouble finding commonalities, look for these possibilities:

> **Context & identity.** They belong to the same group, live in the same neighborhood, are of the same age, or work in the same profession.

> **Similar problems.** These can be personal—financial strain, health issues, high stress at work, raising children alone. Or systemic—living in a troubled neighborhood, working in a declining industry, experiencing similar discrimination, dealing with overburdened or corrupt bureaucracy.

> **Desire for change** in the situation, a hope that the conflict will end, a shared history of trying to make amends.

> **Costs of the conflict.** They may each find the current situation painful, expensive, frustrating, disruptive, confusing, or holding them back from getting on with their lives.

> **Mutual regrets, admissions of fault.**

> **Principles, values, goals,** whatever they've brought up already—a commitment to improving quality control, a similar work ethic, or valuing people's right to privacy. *You both care deeply about doing what's best for your children.*

> **Previous good times.**

> **Shared love for something or someone.** They may both love their profession, their neighborhood, the same football team, their God. They may have children or friends or relatives in common. They may even care about each other.

Scenarios: Emotionally difficult situations

▶ Anguish, crying

➤ Take tears in stride. Pass the tissue box. Sympathize with Dolores in a general way: *That kind of thing can be painful to deal with.* Show by your reactions that crying is a normal part of mediation (which is true).

➤ After her dramatic outburst, try to say very little. Your silence may make room for others to respond in a softened way. It can become a turning point.

➤ Keep in mind other parties may be more irritated than moved—they may see it as a pull for sympathy. If you sense this, avoid seeming to "buy in." Keep an open mind—they may be right!

➤ Don't assume Dolores is in more pain than other participants who may not express it with tears. Ask all parties if they'd like a break.

➤ Ask all parties if they want to approach the topic differently.

➤ Use Separate Conversations to give Dolores a chance to think through what her reaction is about, what she wants to do, and to give others a chance to share their reaction and consider options.

➤ If Dolores wants to continue but isn't ready to be in the same room with the others, consider using shuttle diplomacy until everyone's ready to get back to the table.

▶ New, upsetting information

➤ Ask Ramon if this is new information for him.

➤ If he says yes, gauge his reaction, or ask for his thoughts. If he seems stunned or rattled, acknowledge that it's major news to digest.

➤ Signal Betty to pause. Make space for Ramon to absorb it, comment, ask a question—don't just go on with the mediation as if it can be dealt with later!

➤ Acknowledge the other party too. *It takes courage to be honest,* or simply, *It helps to get this on the table.*

➤ Test direction. Do they want to explore the new information, go on to something else, take a break, end the session and reconvene in a few days? Would Separate Conversations help?

➤ Encourage Ramon not to make big decisions right away.

**6.4
SCENARIO:
ANGUISH, CRYING**

Dolores is distraught, and the rest of the participants are sitting at the table looking embarrassed and not knowing what to say.

**6.5
SCENARIO:
NEW, UPSETTING
INFORMATION**

It's just come out during the Exchange that a long-time colleague Betty, who Ramon considered a close friend, in fact secretly gathered evidence against him and went to the Board of Trustees to get him fired.

(with thanks to Sandi Adams)

Scenarios: Emotionally difficult situations

▶ Possible mental health or addiction issues

Norah is in a panicky rage, shouting that the neighbors are spying on her, and are planning to take away her dogs. The neighbors try to reassure her, but nothing anyone says makes the slightest dent.

You doubt she is together enough to make or keep an agreement.

Even if Norah appears to be dealing with mental illness or addiction, she may still be able to participate in mediation. The question is how fully she seems able to understand the situation, reach an agreement, and follow through.

➤ Take extra time to draw Norah out about what she knows and how she interprets it, to assess whether she is willing or able to take in new information or see things differently.

➤ Project stability, competence, and respect.

➤ Talk with Norah privately about what the neighbors could do that might calm her fears.

➤ Strategize with the neighbors separately. Sometimes the other party understands the difficulty and wants to continue the mediation. *How could you lessen Norah's anxiety so that she is more likely to consider your proposal?* Be the agent of reality: will making the agreement work rest mostly on their shoulders? If so, do they feel it's worth trying anyway?

➤ Avoid diagnosis words ("Norah's behavior seems paranoid"; "Since Norah's an alcoholic…") even if Norah has used those terms about herself. The labeling may feel like a put-down coming from someone else. Or you may hear the other party announce, "Even the mediator thinks your accusations about us are paranoid."

➤ End the session if it's clear that Norah can't function well enough to have conversation or make a decision. Confer privately with her and with the neighbors about options they might pursue.

Scenarios: Emotionally difficult situations

▶ Abiding, overriding anger

➤ Acknowledge Hank's experience and feelings, then ask for information: *Hank, it's clear you are deeply grieved about not seeing your sons regularly.* [To both:] *Is there a court order? What does it say? What's the actual pattern been?* Hank's anger may ebb as these impartial questions reassure him you want the topic addressed.

In a Separate Conversation

➤ Get Hank talking about his needs and the impact on him—instead of about Ginny: *Hank, how has this intense conflict over the children affected your relationship with them?*

➤ Focus on his life goal (time with sons) not his conflict goal (punish ex-wife). *Mediation can't punish. But maybe we can straighten things out enough that you can see your sons more often.*

➤ Ask Hank what he most wants Ginny to understand or do differently, and explore what he could try to make that happen. How can he communicate that at the table or in writing? What can you do as mediator to help them discuss it? Is there a mutual friend who might talk with Ginny about it?

➤ Make sure you give full attention and concern to Ginny when you meet with her, too.

6.7
SCENARIO: ABIDING, OVERRIDING ANGER

Hank is furious at Ginny for turning their sons against him. Hank says point-blank he will never ever forgive her, and has no interest in any discussion or compromise—today or ever. He says he just came to make sure she is punished for what she's done.

▶ Attacks, disrespect, name-calling

➤ Make eye contact with Pam. Signal, *Are you okay with this?* Intervene if she signals back no. *Let's pause here a moment.*

➤ Acknowledge the emotion(s) you sense are driving the outbursts. *Bill, it sounds like you're angry that your own skill level hasn't been recognized, is that true?*

➤ Don't treat Pam as a victim, lest it imply that Bill's attack was effective or that Pam can't stand up for herself. Besides, back in their workplace, she may attack Bill routinely—you don't know.

➤ Go back to neutral informational questions for a bit. *I'm not there, so I'm not sure what's been happening on the ground. Can you explain…* Dive back into factual details—who assigns work, how are overloads handled, what changes has Pam made, what skills does Bill bring to the work?

➤ Once things are calmer, you might raise topics that could build cooperation: *Have there been times when things were going okay?* If yes, ask, *What was it like then?* If no, ask, *When did tensions start?*

6.8
SCENARIO: ATTACKS, DISRESPECT, NAME-CALLING

Pam complains, "Bill can't be bothered working hard. He dumps the whole burden of his assignments back on me."

Bill leans forward. "Stop whining, lady—it's your *&%$ job. They pay you twice as much even though you're utterly incompetent. Go ahead and quit. Make everyone's day!"

FACILITATING THE PROCESS

THE TOOLBOX

7

Facilitating the process

Managing the mediation process can be quite a juggling act! The facilitation methods in this chapter are aimed at maximizing parties' participation and sense of ownership, while still exercising your responsibility for navigating them through a difficult conversation.

It starts with tuning into the participants. Some mediations will need little intervention on your part, and you can let the parties spontaneously move from one topic to the next. Others will need your active guidance to keep from getting stuck in negative interaction patterns.

Impartial facilitation

▶ Facilitating even-handedly

Impartiality means not using your position to favor or disfavor one party over another, for any reason. On a practical level, think of it as giving each person the same opportunity to participate and have what they say considered respectfully.

➤ **Distribute your attention evenly.** Consciously shift your gaze often, even when one person is speaking during a go-round.

➤ **Address each person with the same degree of formality.** [See page 97.]

➤ **Don't infer or imply that one person is the problem**, the victim, the aggressor, the one with a complaint, etc. Keep an open mind.

➤ **Deflect attempts to make you an ally.** ("Wouldn't you be mad if someone did X to you?" "You're a professional, what do you advise?") Reflect back their point rather than indicating your opinion. *What's important here is what you two think.*

▶ Balancing participation

➤ **Check that all have had a chance to weigh in** on each subject.

➤ **Stay alert to their conversation dynamics.** Who interrupts? Who defers? Who do others listen to? Whose input is getting overlooked? When people are overlooked or cut off, bring the conversation back around to ensure they get considered.

➤ **Don't comment** on whether they're talking a lot or a little: Instead, ask questions to draw out the quieter people, or ask someone to pause for a moment then check if other participants want to respond.

➤ **If someone is dominating** and the rest are glazing over, interrupt, summarize, then redirect to another participant:

> *George, you're saying a lot of important things here. It's a lot to absorb. Latisha, what do you think about this suggestion?*

Mixed levels of authority in the room

Making participation "equal" can be tricky. Some people, by personality, authority, or centrality to the situation, may appropriately speak much more than others, or have greater decision power. Your role is to help people make their best choices with the existing context. What's important is that each participant experience the session and your facilitation as "fair."

**7.1
BALANCING
PARTICIPATION**

- *Quentin, I'm curious what you think about this.*

- *I don't think Justin got a chance to answer the question about X.*

- *Sydney, can you hang on a moment while Lynn finishes?*

- *Maria is having trouble getting a word in edgewise here! Let's give her some space.*

Mixed authority levels

- *Pat, this is your clinical specialty— how would these changes work?*

- *Of course this is your decision. What kind of input on protocols would be useful for you?*

- *Let's talk about when notification is required. LuAnn, what's your policy now, and how much flexibility is there?*

Structuring the session

▶ Time frame

➤ **2½–3 hours is a productive session length**, long enough to accomplish a lot, short enough to avoid burnout. Schedule a backup second session in advance so that if they don't finish, the first session won't feel like a failure, and follow-up will happen sooner.

➤ **Space out multiple sessions when possible.** Marathon mediations are not only tiring, they dilute people's ability to think and make good decisions. If sessions must be scheduled back to back, allow several hours' break (a long lunch, an overnight), provide nutritious snacks, have more Separate Conversations, and give people more chances to move around or change seats.

➤ **Set a firm ending time**, and move towards closure 15+ minutes beforehand. This helps people manage their energies and impatience. A firm closing time can also press people to get serious and commit to a decision.

▶ Don't we need some rules here?

Assume that participants will be polite and engaged. Most participants do try to be civil towards each other and responsive to the mediator. Most do want to resolve their situation. Appreciate and support those good intentions by the tone you set, and by caring about their interests.

Avoid suggesting how they should behave towards you or towards each other. ("Let's have a respectful conversation." "So we agree there will be no interrupting?" "Please let Janie speak for herself.") This can feel "talked down to." Similarly, setting ground rules implies that without specific, enforceable instructions the parties might not "behave" or the mediators might lose control.

Two other problems with upfront ground rules are that they usually favor prevailing cultural norms of acceptable behavior which the parties may not share, and that people primed for a fight are easily sidetracked into arguing about process, sapping time and energy from talking about the conflict itself.

Establish guidelines together later, if problems arise. If the way they are talking to each other is making it harder for them to negotiate, stop and consult with them. What would help them keep their discussion on track or make it easier to talk about a sensitive topic?

7.2 **WHERE ARE THEY** **RIGHT NOW?**	### ▶ Choices—where to go next?

7.2
WHERE ARE THEY
RIGHT NOW?

Emotional

• *How are you all feeling right now?*

• *I know X is the sticking point—what would you like to do or discuss before we get to it?*

• *Would you like to talk alone with me before everyone discusses it?*

Process

• *Does your family need some time to consult before we finalize this?*

• *That's a lot of data. Would it help to organize it in some way?*

Problem

• *Are we done with topic X?*

• *Any lingering questions on your mind?*

• *Shall we turn to Ned's concern about Z, or keep discussing Y?*

• *Is anything bothering you that hasn't been covered yet?*

▶ Choices—where to go next?

Mediators face frequent choices, small and large, about the direction of the discussion: Could participants use more time to iron out misunderstandings? What question might open up their thinking? Is it okay that he's off topic again? Should I point out that they seem stuck, or let them recognize it first? Do I need to check in with her privately?

What's the destination?

Before changing direction with a new question, topic, or approach, take a second to ask yourself how you think it will help.

Zoom out briefly to your big-picture mental map of where the parties want to go. Where are they on that map? Are they moving in that direction, and if not, what's getting in the way? What do they need to discuss before moving into the next phase?

Where are the parties right now?

➤ Check out what the participants need and how they are feeling before recommending a next step.

➤ Couple that with recognition of the work they've been engaged in, encouraging them rather than implying that they are "doing it wrong."

> *This has been a fruitful discussion—thanks everyone for giving it your best thinking. Are you ready for the next topic?*

> *This is one of the hardest things to talk through because that event was so upsetting. You've done some good work on it. I'm wondering if you'd like to take a break at this point?*

➤ If you sense people's larger goals and priorities have shifted—for better or for worse—revisit your "map" with them, so that collectively you can reset the direction of the mediation process.

Each choice is an experiment

Don't worry too much about getting it right. There are more factors than you can consciously process in a short time. Your choices may have to be quick, and therefore partly rely on trial and error. If you think you made a "wrong" choice, it's no big deal to simply propose another question, topic, or approach.

When you can be directive

⬢ The continuum: Directing ⬅ ➡ Consulting

For the most part, mediators facilitate in responsive mode, following the participants' lead as to what they most want to talk about, and influencing their direction through setting a tone, asking questions, and all the reflecting and rewording tools that acknowledge what they're saying.

When the boat starts to rock a bit, how firmly should the mediator keep a hand on the tiller? In deciding what comes next, mediators have a range of choices between being directive and full consultation. (See pages 134–35 for how to intervene when the waves get high.)

⬢ Directing

➤ **When things are flowing smoothly.** Although it may seem counterintuitive, the directive style is best when conversations are going well:

✓ You are setting up the next task in a sequence the group is already expecting.

✓ They seem comfortable with your facilitation and engaged in the mediation.

➤ **Save their energies.** Stepping back to decide process questions can distract the participants from the substance of their conversation and tire them out with too many small decisions. If your direction makes sense to them, it is unlikely they will feel controlled or constrained.

➤ **Use a low-key, explanatory tone**, as if you were telling a friend how to find a restaurant. It's not about getting them to listen to you and follow *your* rules. It's about guiding them where they want to go.

➤ **When you need to intervene.** You may also need to be directive when breaking the momentum of a hot conversation, or when someone is feeling attacked. [**See page 103.**] Once you have their attention, if appropriate, you can go into recommendation or consultation mode. [**See next page.**]

⬢ Checking in

Check in with participants to make sure they are okay with the proposed direction, even when you're fairly confident about what should come next. It's a courtesy, and a way to gain commitment. Plus, they may have a better suggestion! If the response seems polite or unenthusiastic, that's your cue to move into consultation mode.

7.3
DIRECTING

- *The next step is coming up with a few options for this topic.*

- *Wait, we've got three topics on the table at once and it's getting confusing. We'll get to that! Joe, you were talking about Y…?*

- *Tania, I think it's your turn.*

- *Let's take the next 10 minutes to wrap up; we'll start with this topic in our next session.*

7.4
CHECKING IN

- *You all seem to have more energy around the hospital incident. Should we look at that next?*

- *Marian has made an offer. I think you're not quite ready to talk about solutions yet. Can we note it and come back to it?*

- *Are you ready to review the final draft now?*

Consulting about direction

The more unhappy parties are with how things are going, the more the mediator needs to consult them about how to move forward. Put yourself in an advisory role, listening and inquiring until they agree on a way forward—or, if they can't, make a recommendation.

Giving choices + recommendation

> **Lay out the two or three best choices** for what to do next. (Be sure you can live with whatever they decide.) Weighing more than three choices can make deciding too stressful. If they don't like any of them, work with them to come up with a new option or two.

> **Say which one you prefer, and explain the pros and cons you see.**

Why limit choices and give your recommendation—doesn't that influence their decision? Yes, you have more knowledge about process than they do, and so your recommendation is a faster way to find something workable. The less time spent on process mechanics, the more energy they have for substantive conversation and decisions.

Conferring about the process

When you're not seeing a clear path forward, stop and tune in to where they are emotionally and mentally, and pause to ask them about the mediation process itself.

> **People:** How are they doing in terms of emotions, energy, optimism? Do they need to "recharge"?

> **Process:** How is the conversation going for them? What might make it more fruitful? Ask what they want to discuss next, what kind of support or guidance they'd like from you.

> **Problem:** Is new information coming out? Are they getting clearer about what matters to each person? Are there uncomfortable concerns that they haven't raised yet? Is their goal for the mediation changing, or their sense of priorities? Do they need to go back to something discussed earlier?

Their responses will let you know whether they want to keep going on the current track or try something different, whether they want to decide what to talk about next, or prefer that you suggest the next step.

7.5
CHOICE WITH RECOMMENDATION

- *I'm not sure everyone's clear yet about what you're proposing. Could you explain it again, or sketch it out on the board? I recommend we take time for clarifying questions before critiquing the idea.*

7.6
DISCUSS THE PROCESS

- *Let's step back a moment and decide how you want to approach this piece.*

- *How could you all discuss this without getting stuck in familiar arguments?*

- *You're all talking at once, and I'm concerned that you may not be able to hear each other. Is there another way to have this conversation?*

Keeping on track

It's normal for groups to stray from the question or topic of the moment. What to do about it depends on why they're off topic, and how tight they expect the agenda and facilitation to be. If a friendly collective reminder, and using the board/chart don't work, try the following:

▶ When they're not engaged

➤ **Find out why the current topic doesn't interest them.** Either reframe the topic or question accordingly to make it more relevant and understandable, or turn to a more immediately compelling topic.

➤ **If the subject only matters to one participant,** "Bill," either ask Bill if it's okay to postpone the topic till later, or look for self-interests that might motivate the "not my problem" participants to address Bill's concern.

➤ **Factor in every participant's needs** before you suggest changing the order or nature of the discussion.

▶ Dog with a bone

When a participant keeps coming back to something over and over, no matter what the current topic is:

➤ **Find out why.** Do they think no one has heard them (probably because no one agreed with them)? Do they consider this topic most urgent? Are they in self-protective mode, and unable to hear anything others say?

➤ **Ask the group** if they would like to talk about the person's concern now. If not, promise to come back to the issue later and ask the person for now, to help the group think about the current topic.

▶ Lively off-topic conversations

➤ Be glad! If all participants seem interested, go with the flow.

➤ If you think the parties may worry about being off-topic, just mention briefly that they've changed direction and that you're fine with it if they are too.

➤ When time is tight, ask them what topics they want to put off until the next session.

➤ If they are making friendly remarks about sports or their kids, recalling past good times, etc., this may be a welcome move towards (re)connecting. Let it go on for a while before suggesting they return to the mediation topics.

7.7
KEEPING THE OPTIONS DISCUSSION ON TRACK

- *Thank you for raising that point. Can we put it on hold for a moment? (Write it on your side list.)*

- *Great, don't lose that! When we're done the salary topic, the Co-op member hours topic is next.*

- *It seems like topics X and Y are connected. Maybe we should think of options for both at the same time?*

Crafting questions

▶ Questions are a fundamental tool

Questions serve many purposes—getting conversation going, showing interest in someone, establishing authority, and getting information, to name a few. When you're facilitating, two purposes are most important:

➤ **Understanding.** A well-crafted and well-placed question helps both the participants and the mediators understand the situation more fully.

➤ **Steering.** Questions direct the conversation. They influence what subjects get attention and validation. They frame how people talk about a topic.

Because asking questions is a directive act that deploys power, questions are sharp tools to use with care. It takes self-conscious practice to develop a sense of what to ask, when, to whom, and how to phrase it.

▶ Question basics

Before you ask, is the question:

➤ **Relevant to resolution?** Do you or the other parties really need to know this information? Would you like them to think about something in a different way? If not, don't ask.

➤ **Centered in *their* reality**? Link to their interests and world view, using language and ideas that make sense to them.

Wording

➤ **Keep 'em short.** It's easy to get long-winded when you're still sorting things through or dealing with a touchy subject. If you find yourself rambling, pause. Then restate in one short and focused sentence.

➤ **One question at a time.** (Sounds obvious, but requires some discipline.)

➤ **Start your questions with "WHAT" or "HOW."** These questions tend to be open-ended, and to invite responses focused on the person's experience. This simple tip is invaluable for constructing questions in the heat of the moment. You'll notice that most examples in this book follow this format.

After you ask

➤ **Listen to the whole reply!**

➤ **Give each party the opportunity to answer.** Discussion sparked by the first reply can distract mediators from giving others their turn.

A request for information doesn't have to be in question form:

- *Oliver, you wanted to comment on option X.*

- *Please fill us in about where your properties are located.*

- *Let's have Walter walk us through the problems he sees with the assessment method.*

For our purposes, invitations and requests are considered one form of "asking questions."

Crafting questions: Word with care

▶ Structuring your questions

Make sure that your questions:

➤ **Stay neutral—don't suggest or persuade.** Avoid questions that start like these: "Have you thought about…?" "Wouldn't it be easier if you could…?" "Have you tried…?" "Wouldn't it be simpler to…?" These efforts to coax the parties are all exhortations or solutions, albeit in polite disguise. A suggestion in question form is still a suggestion! [**See page 161.**]

➤ **Draw out information and interests, rather than demands or positions.** Asking people directly what outcome they want can further harden their positions ("How much are you willing to pay?" "Are you willing to drop the legal claim?" "What would you like her to do?"). Instead, ask, *What would work? How might that help?*

➤ **Don't reflect any one party's view of the situation.** You wouldn't want to turn and ask the accused party, "Why did you cut her out of the meeting?" or "Is there a reason you aren't complying with the bylaws?"

➤ **Can be answered many ways, not just yes or no, A or B.** Binary questions usually start with verbs ("Are your desks in the same room?" "Have you ever asked her about this?"), or with "which." ("Which option do you prefer?) Such questions shrink the number of possible replies and pin people down. For example, *What time that day works for you?* opens up more options than "Does three o'clock work for you?" However, binary or narrowing questions can be a good choice when precise details or firm decisions are needed.

➤ **Use synonyms for "WHY."** For some reason, "why" sentences can sound accusatory in English, as if you are interrogating rather than inquiring. Substitute "what" or "how," (*What led you to…? How did you decide?*) or invitation language (*Could you explain your thinking about…?*).

▶ Asking about a sensitive matter

If you hesitate to ask directly about a sensitive topic, depersonalize it by describing what "some people" in their situation feel or think, followed by a question:

> *Some people in this kind of situation feel that* _____. *What has your experience been?*

> *Caring for an ill person can be very wearing and lonely, and support can mean a lot. What's your sense of what you need?*

Crafting questions: Spin it positive

Use neutral questions early in the mediation: In the beginning, you'll hear complaints. Don't reinforce them with negative questions (What's wrong, what don't they like, what makes them angry) which only solidify their focus on their distress. Instead, ask neutral questions. *What's the situation? Can you give me an example?*

Then shift to positively worded questions once their initial complaints have been aired: *What might help the neighborhood come together on this issue?* Parties may still talk about past injuries, but now the purpose is to get the information they need to take action towards a more palatable future.

THE SHIFT	NEGATIVE ➡	POSITIVE
What doesn't work ➡ what would work better	What problems have come up when you work together? What upsets you about working with Vera?	*What would make it more comfortable for you and Vera to work together?*
Done-unto ➡ proactive	Could you explain what happened to you?	*How did you handle the situation as it unfolded?*
Giving something up ➡ gaining benefits	How would you like to divide up the holidays this year?	*What arrangements would make the holidays happy for your children and manageable for both of you?*
	Are you willing to compromise?	*What trade-offs might help you ensure sufficient funding for your project?*
	How much are you willing to pay?	*You have a chance to put this behind you. Help me get a sense of how much that is worth to you.*
Fixing ➡ creating	What will you do if the agreement breaks down?	*How can you keep communication channels open?*

Crafting questions: Follow up for clarification

Use follow-up questions to help everyone, including the speaker, get a clearer understanding. Take care not to fire off so many questions that they think you're interrogating!

Prompts

> *Could you say more about that?*

> ➤ **When** you want them to keep talking, use a prompt. These short follow-up phrases keep the ball in the air, sometimes with a nudge towards a given direction. [**See sidebar.**]

> ➤ **Be aware** that you're using them, and as with longer questions, think consciously about purpose and direction.

Clarifying questions

There are lots of different questions you can use to clarify what someone has said:

> ➤ **Zoom in** for examples and factual details. *Who owns the house? What did she say in response?*

> ➤ **Zoom out** to put something in context. *Has this happened other times? This rule applies across the board?*

> ➤ **Home in on what prompted feelings and perceptions.**

> *You said this event changed how you felt about him. What was it that made you angry?*

> ➤ **Check out mind-reads.** [**See pages 44, 150.**] *Let's ask Tracey to explain what she intended by that.*

> ➤ **Pull out information** from the interpretation that surrounds it.

> *When you say "she always…," are there times when it doesn't happen?*

> *What was it about the doctor's attitude that upset you?*

> ➤ **Check out ambiguities.** *Did you mean 12 noon or 12 midnight?*

> ➤ **Say it for them.** When you sense what they are wanting to say but can't.

> *So at this point you have given up trying to salvage your partnership, is that what you are saying?*

7.9
FOLLOW-UP PROMPTS TO GET SPECIFICS

- *I see. And then?*

- *So you were sick that week….?*

- *I'm confused, could you sketch that out?*

- *What else did you want to say about this?*

- *Help me understand _____.*

- *Can you give us an example?*

- *How does that relate to _____?*

- *I'm not sure what you mean by _____.*

- *Could you describe what happened when _____?*

- *How did that impact your company?*

- *What were you expecting would happen?*

- *Clearly this has been frustrating for you. Can you say more about how?*

THE TOOLBOX
Facilitating the Process

Kinds of rewording

Reflecting back and other rewording tools, in all their variety, are basic to the mediator craft. The lines between each of these methods are admittedly blurry, and there are no standard definitions. What's important is being able to edit, reframe, organize, and test what you hear, to suit the moment. [**See also page 101.**]

Below are potential mediator responses to this complaint from a production manager: "Your sales department was utterly irresponsible! I can't believe you promised this customer 10,000 customized purple Wacky Widgets with a five-day turnaround and with no change in price!"

METHOD	WHAT TO DO	EXAMPLE
Repeat, highlight	Echo a subset of their words, with a rising intonation to make it a question.	*A 5-day turnaround…? Tell us how that creates problems for you.*
Paraphrase, restate	Repeat back the essence of what someone says, minus their biased or inflammatory words.	*You're saying that Sales contracted with a new customer for 10K customized widgets at the usual price, and with delivery in 5 days, is that right?*
Reflect back, acknowledge	Paraphrase, and include nonverbal and emotional content.	*What's most frustrating to you, then, is the pressure of turnaround promises that your people can't meet, and pricing that doesn't cover your extra costs for overtime and supplies. Did I miss anything?*
Summarize	Organize a number of points or actions into a short, coherent list.	*I think you've raised three concerns: 1) calculating turnaround time, 2) pricing to cover Production's extra expenses, and 3) how Sales and Production can consult more effectively. Did I get them all?*
Reframe	Describe their situation with an alternate interpretation, or reorganize into new categories.	*From what you report, it sounds like your company's current practices can cause disconnects between Sales and Production about deadlines—what the customer needs versus what Production can complete. And you're working off of different pricing formulas. Does that sound right?*

Reflecting back

▶ Reflect back to the speaker

Reflecting back means restating the main points someone has just made, including the emotional content, translated into neutral language. It should always be coupled with looking at them for confirmation, or asking if you got it right. If they correct you, try again till they indicate you've nailed it. [**See also page 101.**]

➤ **Important! Reflect back to the speaker, not the listener:** *Sam, are you saying that it's too risky to pay the full sum up front?* Don't describe Sam's position to the table: "*I think Sam is reluctant to pay because….*" Someone may think you are advocating for Sam, and it is more respectful to let Sam speak for himself.

➤ **If you can't follow what they're saying, take the blame on yourself** even if the participant has been confusing, inarticulate, or just hard to listen to.

> *Sorry Mark, I missed that. Could you say that again?*

▶ When a participant just doesn't "get it"

Reflecting back can be a useful technique when one participant just doesn't seem to understand, much less accept, what another party is saying.

➤ **Face the speaker** and summarize their point of view for the benefit of that "clueless" listener:

> *Mark, if I understand right, you don't intend to close this store, or put Sally out of a job. But you do want to shift toward younger clientele. And you're willing to give Sally an extended contract of some sort. Did I get that right?*

Look mostly at Mark, not at Sally! Use neutral language and tone so as not to put Sally on the defensive. Then get confirmation from Mark that you've summarized correctly. Sally may be better able to hear it coming from you, in this indirect way. (At the same time, don't forget, Sally may be disbelieving for a good reason. Mark may be lying.)

➤ **Be wary of asking people to restate the other party's point of view;** in a mediation context, they are likely to find it distasteful and coercive.

**7.10
REFLECTING BACK
EXAMPLES**

- *Ella, as I understand it, your main concern is getting fair reimbursement for the damage to your windows. And you've been frustrated by the interactions you and Sam have had so far, is that right?*

- *Sam, you are reluctant to pay because you don't think it was your fault? You say you've been losing patience and would like to see this situation over and done with?* [Sam confirms with a nod.] *Anything else on your mind at this point?*

Summarizing

▶ Purpose: To put things in order

A summary distills, categorizes, and orders key points of the discussion in a list. It should simplify enough that participants can wrap their minds around a set of information. The Topic List is a classic example of a summary. [**See page 61.**]

You can summarize lots of things—whenever there are enough elements that organizing them will help people keep track:

- Concerns
- Interests
- Criteria
- Opinions
- Topics
- Options
- Progress to date
- Information
- Work/info needed
- Points of agreement
- Plans, schedules

▶ Summarizing basics

Summarizing needs to be succinct and impartial.

➤ **Select the most important points.** The mediator's opinion and judgment comes into play here to some extent, because you'll necessarily decide what details to leave out, as well as how to prioritize and frame the items. However, do not add in new content or your own opinions.

➤ **One sentence or phrase per item.** It's a list, not a speech.

➤ **Five or fewer items.** If you have more, subgroup them into categories. The goal is for people to wrap their minds around all of the key points at once.

➤ **Use tactful and positive language.** [**See pages 152–55.**]

➤ **Downplay "ownership" of ideas and concerns.** Instead of reviewing Dick's points followed by Anne's points, summarize the situation as a whole: the topics they need to address, the interests they want to meet, the progress they have already made.

➤ **Always end with a request for additions and corrections.**

If you stumble trying to tidy up your words and ideas the first time, the participants often won't notice. Just wait till you're clearer, and try again a few minutes later.

7.11
SAMPLE SUMMARIES

Collect their concerns.

Let's see where we are. I have heard concerns about applying the Homeowner Association renovation rules, about who pays for empty units, and also who can have access to the books and meetings.

What other concerns am I missing?

Organize information the group has covered

To summarize, we've heard about how this has affected the children—being afraid to ride the bus, name-calling, some stone throwing.

But we haven't yet heard much about how the situation is affecting the parents.

Should we look at that question next?

Summarizing: Its many uses

▶ Buy time! When in doubt...SUMMARIZE

Summarizing belongs in the top tray of your toolbox. It serves many purposes on all three sides of the triangle:

People

➤ **Show that you took in what they have to say** and that you empathize.

➤ **Reframe concerns and information** to be more relevant and legitimate to the other parties.

➤ **Sort out their intended message** when you don't follow what they're saying. Confusion is your friend! You don't have to have a neatly organized list in your head before you attempt to summarize. When you ask participants what you're missing, they'll help you out.

➤ **Point out their commonalities,** mutual interests, areas of agreement.

Process

➤ **Structure and focus subsequent discussion.**

➤ **Buy yourself time to think** about where to go next. Summarizing is a good filler for blank moments.

➤ **Reinforce the progress they've made.**

> *You're making headway here. You've cleared up a few important misunderstandings AND you've reached several points of agreement already: 1, 2, 3...*

➤ **Tie up loose ends** and connect the discussion to the next topic.

> *Okay, so what's left is the property line issue, with questions about both the easement and the surveyor's report.*

Problem

➤ **Foreground, cluster, or reframe** significant points. Summarizing always involves editing—what details to include or overlook—and judgments about how to connect different ideas and perspectives.

➤ **Organize information** so people can see the whole, not just the parts.

➤ **Review areas of agreement and disagreement,** work left to do.

Working visually

⬤ Discussion made visible

Record the discussion's main points on a board or flip chart if you can. It's an invaluable aid for tracking and recalling the discussion.

Another benefit—jointly facing the board can be less stressful than looking at each other. And adding a concern to a list may feel less aggressive than making a direct accusation or demand.

Confidentiality alert: Stipulate at the start of the mediation that only mediators may photograph the board.

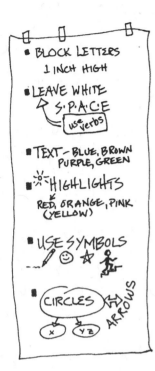

⬤ Tips for using a flip chart or board

➤ **Treat the board as neutral territory**, a work zone where participants can puzzle through their conflict together.

- Write up concerns, interests, and ideas without tagging them as belonging to one party or person.

- Use their language, their key words, and their metaphors—as long as those terms are tactful and mutual.

➤ **Use visuals to direct the discussion.** *Let's talk about this list of key concerns now, and save that list for later…*

➤ **Make progress and hope visible**. Jot down anything they agree about, to serve as motivator and reminder.

Think physically

If the participants or the conversation seem to be lagging, find an excuse to get them to stand up and demonstrate something. Or, to help them explore options, hand each of them a marker and invite them to add their thoughts to the board, to highlight, draw connections, rearrange.

Think graphically

Don't just use the board to make lists! Pictures and diagrams are a great way to work with information and to solve problems. [**See page 162.**] Some uses include:

➤ Explanations (sketch their office layout, diagram their relationships, organization chart).

➤ Organizing and comparing complex information or options (grids, graphs, concept maps).

➤ Sequencing (schedules, flow chart, project planning, calendar).

When to intervene

▶ Is their conversation productive?

The conversation is painful, they are too angry to listen, they've fallen back into a cycle of attack-defend. Should you intervene? In deciding whether to interrupt and change the style or direction of discussion, the basic measures are:

1. Are they learning from each other?

2. Is the level of hostility trending down rather than up?

A discussion can still be productive even when the parties are loud or rude or upset, or they are all talking at the same time. As long as the two criteria above seem true, put up with your own discomfort as far as you can. Otherwise, step in—animosity can escalate fast.

PRODUCTIVE	UNPRODUCTIVE
✓ The parties are responding to each other (whatever the volume!).	✓ They aren't taking in what the other person is saying except to justify their outrage or as ammunition for counterattack.
✓ Everyone is contributing to the discussion.	✓ Someone has withdrawn from participating.
✓ The parties seem to take accusations and emotional language in stride.	✓ Their put-downs seem gratuitous or wounding.
✓ Information new to them is coming out. ✓ Misunderstandings are being aired.	✓ Someone keeps rehashing a subject that has been thoroughly discussed. ✓ They're complaining at length but can't seem to turn that into interests or options.
✓ The subject of discussion seems vital to them even if it seems irrelevant or off-track to you.	✓ They're sidetracked onto unhelpful topics, or avoiding important ones. ✓ They are bogged down in too much detail and long stories.
✓ You sense that one party is approaching a turning point—getting ready to apologize, recognize the other person's situation, make a concession.	✓ They're locked in a cycle of accusation and defense, fixated on who is to blame and what "really" happened.

When to intervene: Stopping the momentum

STOP THE MOMENTUM

SLOW THINGS DOWN

PROCEED IN A NEW WAY OR IN A NEW DIRECTION

At times, despite your best efforts, the conversation melts down. **Step in!** Don't let it continue in hopes it will work itself out. Displays of hostility can quickly pick up speed, and backing down becomes harder.

First, you need to interrupt the escalation of noise and overwrought emotion, get their attention, then hold it long enough to give them time to cool off before you restart the discussion.

▶ Break the momentum

Here are several strategies for interrupting, from gentle to forceful. Note that when people are shouting, your gestures and body position communicate better than your words.

➢ **Use people's names**, and try to catch their eye.

➢ **Acknowledge that you are interrupting.**

> *Hang on a second, I'm not sure I'm following you.*
>
> *Let me interrupt you for a moment.*
>
> Make a "time out" gesture.

➢ **Ask the quieter person to pause.** This takes one voice out of the fray.

> *Jim, can you hold off for a minute? That would be helpful — thanks.*

➢ **Use a few commanding words** (not a stream of them!). Do it once quietly to see if they pay attention. If not, raise your voice. Be firm but unperturbed.

> *Time out!*
>
> *Excuse me: Victor! Kate! Stop!*

➢ **Stand up and move deliberately.** One calming option is to slowly move close to the person who is dominating, while continuing to look at the other party. When you stand up, or come between them, do it with authority.

➢ **Make a SHARP change** in your voice or position — surprise them.

➢ **Quietly ask the less agitated party to step out of the room** for a minute to help defuse the situation.

➢ **Call for a break**, followed by Separate Conversations.

When to intervene: Slowing the process down

The pivotal moment is those few seconds of silence after you have gotten their attention.

➤ **Slow yourself down:** your speaking pace, your gestures. Breathe! But keep a large presence.

➤ **Acknowledge their strong emotion** but don't go back into discussion, much less raise the subject of their argument yet.

> *Phew! Feelings are running high right now. Respect is a big issue for all of you. I'm still unclear about a few things.... But first, let's take a break.*

➤ **Speak personally and kindly** to each of them in a tone that helps bring their heart rate down and cool their defensiveness.

➤ **Slow them down** with strategies such as:

- Activity: Put a fresh sheet up on the flip chart, refill their water glasses.

- Talk about whatever: Summarize. Review what they've accomplished already. Sympathize.

- Ask the quieter participant an innocuous question.

- Take a break.

➤ **This is not a teachable moment.** Be careful not to scold or advise.

▶ Starting back up

Don't make them "wrong"

➤ **Dampen your own irritation or nervousness:** Tell yourself: "They're stuck and frustrated—how can I help them cool down and feel less defensive?"

➤ **Frame the argument as a process breakdown**, not as their bad behavior.

➤ **Take the blame.** Don't make them "wrong." Instead of pointing out what they are doing ("You're all talking at once!" or "You're just repeating yourselves here"), start with your *own* responsibility or confusion.

Redirect

Ask if they're willing to try something different. Restart discussion with a different approach or different topic than the one they exploded over before. Discuss (together or separately) what would help them be able to really hear each other, and how they could communicate so that the other party "gets it."

7.12
FRAME IT AS PROCESS

- *This isn't working—let's come at it from another direction.*

- *I can see we're all a bit weary. You're raising important things, and I wonder if we should tackle this again in next week's session.*

7.13
BLAME YOURSELF

- *Let's pause for a second—I need to catch up here.*

- *Sorry, I'm confused. Can we step back and have each of you give me a specific example of what's going on?*

- *Let me see if I can make the question more specific this time.*

Is it time to quit?

▶ Reasons to end the mediation

In deciding whether to end a mediation, consider the following:

1. Are they capable of participating productively?

- No amount of explanation resolves a person's confusion.

- Someone persists in threatening or disrupting.

- Someone keeps repeating their accusations and demands, even when the group has reassured and accommodated them.

- One party seems to have no interest in resolution, or is attending as a tactic (to buy time, to get information, to please the judge).

- Someone seems to have taken drugs or alcohol before the session.

2. Is mediation the best approach or forum?

- One or more parties do not want to continue the mediation.

- Even after working together a while, their desires and goals remain unrealistic, unreachable, or miles apart.

- Needed information is not and will not be available.

- It turns out that they need other stakeholders or authorized decision-makers at the table to make any headway.

- You are not the right mediator (for whatever reason), or this is not the right time for mediation.

3. Could continuing the mediation endanger someone?

Occasionally, you will sense that continuing to mediate could be dangerous for some participants, for the organization, or for the community. [**See page 103.**]

- Someone may retaliate after the mediation.

- One party appears to be gathering information to be used against the other party (in court, to fire them, etc.) or to justify retaliation.

- Someone is using mediation as a way to keep illegal or dangerous behavior under cover, to avoid public sanction or punishment.

- The solutions they are proposing are illegal, or unethical (in your judgment), or might harm people who aren't represented at the mediation.

Ending a mediation

▶ They want to quit

When a party wants to break off the mediation, and it seems to be a firm decision, assure them that participation is voluntary and that they have no obligation to stay. Then ask if you can speak with them separately before they leave. Potential topics of conversation:

✓ Concerns they have — about you, about the process, about the other party, about what has been said, or about proposed agreements.

✓ What other options they have, and the potential fallout of stopping.

✓ Whether a partial or time-limited agreement would be useful and acceptable.

✓ If they are willing to have a joint and orderly closing with the other party present (to make future interactions easier).

Ultimately, if people want to quit the mediation or take their problem elsewhere, that is their choice. Be gracious.

▶ You decide it's time to stop

Don't hesitate to end a mediation if **you** don't feel comfortable continuing, for whatever reason. [**See page 168.**]

➤ **Be sensitive to the participants' interpretations** of why you are ending the mediation. For instance, don't end abruptly following a Separate Conversation or one party's outburst, leaving others to imagine what was said privately or thinking that the mediator found one party impossible to handle.

➤ **Give vague, general reasons** that don't even hint at blame.

➤ **Treat each participant politely.** Remember that even if you hear convincing accounts about wrongdoing or abuse, participants are almost certainly giving you an incomplete and skewed picture.

➤ **Let them know about other available resources.** You may want to do this privately at the end, or call them later.

➤ **Validate the work they have done**, what they've learned. Thank them for giving it a try, and wish them well.

7.14
SAMPLE EXITS

- *Since the people we need in the room to make or uphold an agreement aren't here, I suggest we end this mediation.*

- *Based on what I've heard, it sounds to me like mediation is not the right forum for this situation. If you would like some assistance on where to go next, I'd be happy to talk with you by phone this week.*

- *I don't think I can be of help to you here, at least until you've each consulted a lawyer.*

- *I've concluded that you would do better with a mediator who specializes in this particular area. I can give you a referral, if you like.*

THE TOOLBOX
Facilitating the Process

Scenarios: Facilitation challenges

▶ Arriving with a friend or lawyer

> ➤ Ask Rex and the lawyer to step out of the room to speak with you. Point out that Rex had agreed in advance about who will be attending. Ask them to come back into the room to reschedule and to discuss whether Rex's lawyer can attend that meeting or not.

> ➤ At the table, explain that you recommend postponing the session. If Colleen immediately says she wants to go ahead today, ask if she would feel more comfortable if the lawyer was not present, as per their initial agreement.

> ➤ If she wants the lawyer to leave, ask Rex whether he's okay with that. If not, insist on rescheduling, and have them discuss who will attend.

> ➤ If she says it is not a problem, get clear agreement about how the lawyer can participate—in keeping with guidelines you think essential (e.g., that the lawyer can consult with Rex anytime, but cannot speak for him or ask Colleen questions directly; or that Rex has pledged to make full financial disclosure and you expect the lawyer to honor that).

▶ Accusing the mediators

> ➤ Be grateful that Richard accused you out loud, because now you can address the problem (whether or not it has much to do with you). *Thanks for giving me that feedback, Richard.*

> ➤ Express regret. *I'm sorry my style isn't working for you.*

> ➤ Ask Richard what upset him. Then ask Kyle if he has similar concerns.

> ➤ Don't explain or justify how you've facilitated. Talk about what's next: how you propose to facilitate in light of their concerns.

> > *You want to make sure I give you time to fully explain what happened, and you want me to understand that you feel strongly about protecting your reputation—is that right?*

> ➤ Connect Richard's complaints and emotions with his interests:

> > *Maybe you are worried that this conversation could actually prompt Kyle to retaliate later?*

> > *You want to make sure that everyone here believes you, and recognizes your authority in this matter.*

7.15
SCENARIO: ARRIVING WITH A FRIEND OR LAWYER

Colleen's contractor, Rex, arrives late with his lawyer in tow, and they sit down immediately and spread their papers along one side of the table. You had a verbal understanding that only Rex and Colleen would be there.

7.16
SCENARIO: ACCUSING THE MEDIATORS

All of a sudden, Richard lashes back at you, saying you are prejudiced against him. "You all are nice ladies, but Kyle is just using you." You think your remarks have been impartial and gentle, so you are at a loss for a response.

138

The Mediator's Handbook

Scenarios: Facilitation challenges

➡ The silent one

➤ Ask Silas a few short-answer questions about plain facts to break the ice, then a longer one about something he likes. How long has he owned the car? Does he use it to get to work? What's fun about driving it?

➤ Guess about Silas's unspoken feelings and needs, using a depersonalized description, then end with a confirmation question:

> *I'm guessing it's frustrating to listen to this and figure you don't have much chance of getting your car back no matter what anyone does. Is that right?*

➤ Talk about his silence directly:

> *Silas, we want to find out what might make things go better for you as well. Can you tell us what's getting in the way of talking about it?*

➤ If he still can't, then break for Separate Conversations.

In Separate Conversations

➤ Tell Silas what you observed in a tone of interest and concern, and offer an open-ended question.

> *You haven't been saying very much, and I just wanted to check in to see what you're thinking and feeling.*

> *It looks like you're really angry. Can you tell me what's going on? Is there anything I can do to make it easier for you to take part?*

➤ If he still does not open up, ask him if he has any concerns about the mediators or the mediation process.

➤ If he says no, help him explore what he might lose by staying silent.

> *Barbara can't be the only one who decides the terms of the agreement. It's okay to end the mediation, if you think something else will work better for you. What do you see your options as right now?*

➤ In a Separate Conversation with Barbara, explore ways she can help make it easier for Silas to speak his mind.

7.17
SCENARIO: THE SILENT ONES

Ever since Barbara lit into him, Silas has been sitting with his arms folded and won't say a word. When you ask him questions or offer him a chance to speak, he just says, "I have nothing else to say."

Scenarios: Facilitation challenges

7.18
SCENARIO:
BREAKING UP A
SHOUTING MATCH

Every few minutes, either Claudia or Pablo explodes with anger and shouts that the other person's name-calling is offensive, that they never should have agreed to come to mediation, it's a waste of time. Now Pablo is calling Claudia a racist and Pablo's wife has joined in the fray.

▶ Breaking up a shouting match

➢ Interrupt. Make eye contact with each of them, and use their names. *Claudia, Pablo, stop now!*

➢ If they continue to shout, make a sharp change, so they notice you.

➢ *Let's all just take a breath for a moment.* Take one yourself. Lower your voice, slow your movements, and show caring attention.

➢ Emphasize that you want to change gears, that the reason they're here is to try something different.

> *Let's regroup here. You've both said you're under stress and really need things to change. Let's try something different. I'd like to meet with each of you separately, then try a different approach to this when we come back together.*

➢ Or take a cool-off break first, and check in with each of them before reconvening. *We'll take a brief break now, and when we come back…*

➢ Remind yourself that Claudia and Pablo are not "difficult people." They are "people in difficulty" in need of what the Nonviolent Communication community calls "emergency empathy." [**See pages 134–35.**]

7.19
SCENARIO: I'M
OUTTA HERE

Jacquie announces, "I'm outta here," and stalks out of the room. Now the McBickers are saying, "That's it. This whole thing is point-less, we're leaving too!"

▶ I'm OUTTA here

➢ Ask the McBickers to wait until you come back, and follow Jacquie out of the room. Try to persuade her to talk with you for a moment.

➢ Don't exhort Jacquie to stay. *Jacquie, you're free to leave, if that's what is best for you.*

➢ Get Jacquie talking. *Before you go, though, could you talk for a minute about what frustrated you?* People often leave the table because of emotional overload rather than deliberate decision. Once you can get them talking for a while, most people continue with the mediation.

➢ Ask, *What would it take for you to continue?*

➢ Help Jacquie think through the trade-offs of staying or leaving. Which does she think will bring her a better outcome?

➢ Suggest that Jacquie and the McBickers give it another half hour, and if they are still dissatisfied at that point, you will end the session.

SOLVING THE PROBLEM

THE TOOLBOX

8

Participants' starting point: Power & rights

Mediation is for dilemmas where people can't get what they want without each other's cooperation, yet they have gotten stuck in adversarial mode. They often default to adversarial strategies like exerting power and appealing to "rights." Once they get to mediation, they may continue to use these strategies until their understanding of the situation starts to shift.

▶ Power to help or harm

Power-based tactics are usually "carrots" to buy someone's cooperation or "sticks" that threaten harm and impose costs. These in turn reinforce adversarial responses and bad feeling, even if superficially they produce agreement. Typical power tactics during mediation are:

✓ Dominating—threatening, shouting, lecturing, constantly interrupting, standing up.

✓ Manipulating—cajoling, flattering, bribing.

✓ Posturing—taking outsized positions to get attention, to lower the other parties' expectations, or to make room for later concessions.

✓ Goading—insulting, taunting, sneering, demeaning, baiting—to throw the adversary off balance, make them lose their cool.

✓ Pressuring—asserting authority, using one's power base, marshaling allies, name-dropping, threatening the adversary's reputation.

✓ Deceiving—lying or withholding information, revealing confidences.

▶ Appeal to rights

Laws, rules, policies, principles, social norms—disputing parties call on these social and institutional "rights" to help protect themselves and to get cooperation. Victory may bring finality, legitimacy, and enforcement, but results may be uncertain and slow. In determining winners and losers, the outcome may also fuel a new round of conflict.

✓ Presenting evidence and justifications to support one's case.

✓ Defining the conflict based on how the law might define and judge it. ("They are harassing us!" "Regulatory compliance is required.")

✓ Presenting oneself as respectable, well-intentioned, victimized, having legitimate claims. Painting the other as immoral, guilty, selfish, unkind.

✓ Hiding or collecting information with an eye towards a lawsuit.

Changing the "positions" mindset

▶ Positions = premature solutions

"Either you fire her, or I'm out of here."

"No one gets special treatment in this organization."

"The kids must live with me full time. That's non-negotiable."

A party's "position" or stance at the start of a mediation — their demands or requests, their ideas about how to settle the conflict — are their protective armor. These positions are backed up, implicitly or explicitly, by threats or promises.

Taking a strong position can force the other parties to deal with the conflict. In this case, parties may cling tightly to their well-rehearsed demands, and fear they will lose face or lose protection if they back down.

Most positions are one-sided or premature solutions to a half-understood problem. Because parties are operating on incomplete information about the other parties, their proposed solutions are likely to be unrealistic. Or they may be designed to fix a problem that proves not to be the real problem after all.

▶ Redirect towards sharing information

The mediator's job is to change the conversation from a standoff between dueling positions to a discussion of how the parties can meet their interests.

➤ **Concentrate on information and interests.** Instead of getting them to ease up on their positions and strategies, patiently work to bring out useful information, maintaining an attitude of caring and curiosity about their needs.

➤ **Don't get distracted** by the parties' power and rights mindset or by strong position-taking. It's a theatrical sound-and-light show that won't lead them to a solid resolution.

➤ **Give them time to shift gears.** Interest-based problem-solving means both listening *and* sharing — more than participants may be ready for. Try to create an emotionally supportive atmosphere that helps them to weather criticisms, to hear or tell uncomfortable facts. They are likely to take that risk gradually if they see hope of a resolution.

➤ **Explore the passions behind their positions.** Positions may be rooted in the person's sense of identity and world view — putting forth a deeply felt conviction, not just a tactical proposal. [See page 109.]

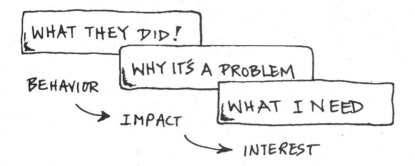

Facilitating the movement from

Distress ➡ Specifics about problem behavior ➡ Impacts ➡ to Needs

is the heavy lifting the mediator does during the session. It's the work that brings interests into focus, and sets the stage for problem-solving.

▶ Interests = what matters and why

Interests are the needs and wants that motivate someone, the benefits that people are protecting or seeking. Each person will have many interests, some of them contradictory, some of them not fully recognized by the person themselves:

- **Immediate, and specific to the situation:** "I need an employee who can handle the data analysis without much oversight."

- **Long-term:** "I want to raise my kids. I want them to have consistent, responsible parenting." "I want to protect my reputation."

- **Public, visible:** "Our business will suffer until the road is repaired." "I just want to make my own decisions."

- **Private or secret:** "I don't want to be found out." "I want to get out of here, but can't say anything until I find another job."

- **Emotional/social:** "I want the satisfaction of seeing them punished." "I want to do things my way." "I need companionship." "I want my co-workers to respect my competence." "I want to be in charge." "I want to be seen as a reasonable and caring person."

"Interest" is a dry word for passionate matters. Interests are the fire in your belly. The desire to be treated kindly. The fantasy of living unconstrained by other people, of easing out the thorn in your heart.

8.1
**QUESTIONS THAT
GET AT INTERESTS**

- *Why is this upsetting?*

- *What makes this a
  problem for you?*

- *What matters most?*

- *What has brought you
  to care about this so
  much?*

- *What led you to
  decide to do X?*

- *What keeps you from
  leaving?*

- *What's your priority?*

Layers of interests

▶ Many interests at once

When you dig into a concern, you're likely to bring up several layers of interests—from relatively predictable and public ones, to ones that are strategically or emotionally sensitive. For example, say a couple is arguing about whether to vacation in the mountains or at the ocean…

At first you may take their argument at face value and think that Sue loves being in the mountains, while Bob prefers beaches.

Then you find out that she really loves to hike, which she can't do at the beach, while he just wants to relax someplace warm and do nothing.

Digging deeper, you discover that Sue is interested in winning this argument because she gave in to Bob the last two years. Meanwhile, he wants them to have time alone and going to the mountains means visiting her family.

And some interests are so private, the mediators can only guess at them—for example, Sue may take Bob's willingness to accommodate her wishes as a measure of how much he still loves her.

All of these levels are "interests." All may be simultaneously true.

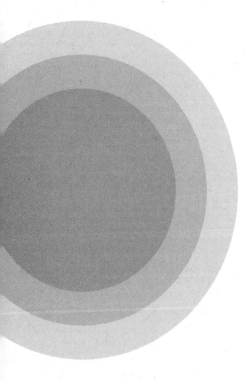

▶ Levels of intervention

Different conflict interveners respond to different layers of interests.

➤ "Stop them from mistreating me!" ➡ Authorities, such as police and courts, and sometimes supervisors or parents, tend to deal with the outer layers, the immediate and visible needs that can be mitigated by intervention.

➤ "I just want to know I belong." ➡ Therapists and ministers help people in conflict deal with their own psychological and spiritual needs.

➤ "I want this situation to change." ➡ Mediators work in the middle layers, looking at relationships and systems, not just the immediate problem. If you think talking about their deeper interests may help them reach resolution, invite people to open up further in a way that they can easily decline. You could address everyone rather than a particular person, use Separate Conversations, or ask, *Is there anything else you want to say now about what makes this a problem?*

Why interests matter

⏵ What mediators can do with interests

Why the unwavering focus on interests? Interests are the fulcrum of the whole mediation process. They contain the information that helps systems and relationships learn and grow. They are the basis for problem-solving and making decisions.

Focusing on the parties' interests can move the mediation forward on each side of the conflict triangle:

People

✓ Educate the other parties and the mediators about the complexity and context of problems that people are dealing with.

✓ Summarize a person's hopes and needs minus the emotional coloration and demands that make it hard for the other party to listen or accept.

✓ Increase people's willingness to care about the needs of the other participants (for example, when they hear reasonable requests, someone else's heartfelt pain, or what else is happening in someone's life).

Process

✓ Provide a focal point for conversation. The goal of "finding out what matters to each person" helps everyone at the table know what to listen for, how to sort it out, and how to understand what gets priority.

✓ Keep participants involved. When you understand what motivates each participant, you can help them stay engaged in the mediation.

Problem

✓ Define the problem in a way that opens up a range of potential solutions.

✓ Articulate, clarify, and legitimize people's needs and wants.

✓ Identify what criteria a successful agreement will need to meet.

✓ Frame their needs as mutual problems, increasing motivation to work together on resolving them.

**8.2
USEFUL INTERESTS**

As we wrote in Chapter 1, of all their interests, the mediator is looking for those which:

✓ Motivate participants' behavior—both at the table and in the future.

✓ Describe a positive state the participant hopes for (= need fulfilled).

✓ Can potentially be resolved through actions participants can take themselves.

Finding space for solutions

▶ How many potential solutions?

The mediator is looking to frame people's interests and topics in a way that creates space for imaginative problem-solving, a space where several options might answer people's needs.

✓ **Meaningful action is possible**, i.e., people can actually do something about the problem.

✓ **You can imagine several potential solutions** — but not dozens — that would be overwhelming! Ideally, each party has room to move, more than one action they might take.

✓ **Fresh, unstuck:** The interest or topic is outlined at a broader or more concrete level than they haven't considered before.

Note: The following examples are for framing interests. For similar thinking about how to frame topics, see pages 61–62.

Zoom in: From a broad interest ➡ to more specific

Broad interests are useful for creating a spirit of cooperation (*You all share an interest in the success of this Mongo Project*). They may not give much guidance for problem-solving, as there can be too many potential solutions to consider and too few criteria to help choose. A more useful level of specificity might be: *You'd like a common measure of "success" for deciding how long to continue the project.* General psychological interests — *John needs to feel safe in his home* — pose the same problem: How to know what will make John feel safe? Try something like, *John wants control over who enters his house.*

Zoom out: From a surface interest ➡ to more encompassing

Narrowly conceived interests tend to sound more like positions — *Jane needs complete expense reports by 1pm each Friday before she processes the payroll.* This level of specificity makes it harder to find a solution that the other party is willing to do than would a somewhat wider interest, such as: *Jane would like a system for expense reports that doesn't require her to chase people down.*

Like Goldilocks, you may find just the right level of interests to discuss. But if you don't, you can always steer towards or away from specifics during the conversation as the resolvable interest becomes clearer.

- Mae: "I want some appreciation for what I have done for this company." (Her manager probably has no clue how to fill this need.)

- *What kind of "appreciation" do you mean?*

- Mae: "They refuse to accommodate my injury…!" (Manager may still not know what is needed or sufficient. Mediator then explores how her injury impacts her work.)

- *Could you tell us more about how your injury affects your work?* (Explore Mae's answer thoroughly.)

- ➡ *So Mae, you need work conditions that don't require sitting for long periods?* (Now the company has possible remedies they can implement.)

Reframing

Reframing means offering a new perspective that might help parties think or feel differently. For example, was the other party "rude" to "ignore" her, or had an authority forbidden him to make contact with her? Are recent small improvements cause for discouragement, or a sign of hope? Reframing is like turning on a spotlight that reveals new elements and changes the color.

▶ Many techniques

Many techniques in this book can be used to do reframing, most notably:

- **Rewording** of all kinds, including drafting the Topic List and summarizing interests, because the mediator is selecting, ordering, and "neutralizing" what was said. [**See page 128.**]

- **Checking out interpretations.** [**See page 44.**]

- **Plain, tactful descriptions**, finding out more information. [**See, e.g., pages 152–53.**]

- **"Flipping it"**—turning negatives from the past into wishes for a positive future. [**See, e.g., page 154.**]

▶ Metaphors

One key reframing technique is noticing and using metaphors. Notice what words a participant uses to explain their own behavior and the other party's. What metaphors might those words represent, and how might they they shape the person's views and behavior?

➤ **Common metaphors that come up:** human nature, sports, warfare, morality, courtroom, victim-protector-perpetrator, the "good" (mother, neighbor, employee, etc.), struggle, psychology, trials of the soul, crime and punishment, animal or less-than-human nature, the classroom.

➤ **Turn their own metaphors in a new direction:** If the situation is a "mess," what needs cleaning up, or organizing? If the other side is "immoral" or "misbehaving," what changes might help everyone to "do the right thing?"

➤ **Introduce another metaphor:** If Kareem sees himself as a victim who is protecting his family, you might recast this as an opportunity to build community alliances. If Todd sees Ben as a "criminal," you might downshift to a less fraught "game" metaphor—recasting Ben as "playing hard for his team." If June and Ricardo speak of "right" and "wrong," make it about a puzzle or system, instead: *What would work? How can this be fixed?*

8.4
REFRAMING WITH METAPHORS

Use their metaphor

- *You feel you've been struggling with this for a long time and have come to a stalemate. I think it shows that you are each able to hold your own! If you can figure out a plan that works for both of you, that strength and persistence could really help change things around.*

Use a different one

- [If they are upset by a "personality clash"] *The daily irritations you describe seem like the weeds that pop up in any organization, which if you prepare the soil, and do a bit of weeding each week, may not get out of hand. How can each of you flourish here?*

149

Checking out (mis)interpretations

▶ What's an "interpretation"?

Interpretations are the meanings a person attaches to events or behavior. Participants don't just object to behavior; they often object to (what they assume are) each other's motives and intentions. Checking out these assumptions can clear up misunderstandings. Even worries confirmed are easier to deal with, and responses disbelieved can open needed discussion on the source of that mistrust.

TYPE OF INTERPRETATION	WAYS TO RESPOND	CHECKING IT OUT
MIND-READS Assumptions about what another person thinks, feels, or intends when they haven't said so directly. "William despises us."	Pause to check with the other party in an easy tone that does not put either person on the defensive. Or ask the speaker why it upsets them.	*Kathy, let's check that out. William, would you be willing to tell Kathy whether her sense of what you're feeling is accurate?* *Kathy, what is the impact on you if William thinks negatively of you?*
WORRIES **#1 What the other party might do.** "If I don't sign this, they'll fire me." "She'll use my child-support money to buy stuff for herself."	Note out loud that the person is making a *prediction*. It may be well-founded, but it is not yet a "fact." Ask what they're experiencing NOW that leads them to predict what might happen next. Check out its accuracy with the other party.	*So Emma, you're predicting that you might get fired? Mel, would you be willing to tell Emma what actions in this situation might put her job at risk?* *Ginny, can you give us a sense of what expenses child support is covering now?*
#2 External consequences. "If you double the fees, we'll lose customers and go bankrupt."		*What information and experiences lead you to worry about the effect of fees or the possibility of bankruptcy?*
ACCUSATIONS "He's been secretly talking to our funders and telling them lies."	Try to ascertain what is observed fact and what is inference. Treat the latter as you would a mind-read. Be careful not to set up a yes-you-did-no-I-didn't argument. Studiously avoid "whodunit," and focus instead on impacts.	*Vicki, what observations led you to think that is happening?* *Vicki, what impact have you experienced? What fallout are you worried about?* *Mike, any information you'd like to clarify here?*

[See page 44.]

Lies, perceptions, deceptions

➡️ "Liar!" Different versions of reality

Nothing seems to cause greater rage than when someone feels that the other party is blatantly lying or falsely accusing them. It can explode the mediation.

Over time, most parties become invested in their own well-rehearsed version of "what happened." Guesses about the other party's motivations become "facts." When accounts clash, it affects trust. If the other party seems dishonest, it is risky to speak openly or to make an agreement.

➤ **Emphasize their power to determine how things will be** from now on, even if they can't agree on what happened or who is at fault.

➤ **Explain that conflicting memories are quite normal,** and hearing what the other party believes can be useful, even if it may be wrong. However, don't try to smooth over ugly facts or egregious behavior in an attempt to make a "nicer" story about what happened.

➤ **Take a mild interest in the evidence they've brought,** but keep your attention on the basics: feelings, information, interests, and options.

➤ **Help them plan ways to confirm those disputed facts** which potentially influence the terms of agreement (e.g., survey a property line, track time spent on tasks, get copies of a relevant ordinance).

➤ **Be clear what mediation can and cannot determine.** [See pages 43, 173.]

➡️ Strategic deception

Of course, people sometimes lie in mediation, and mediators have no way to prove who is telling the truth. But you can try to provide a forum where people don't need to lie to get what they want. Be alert to situations where parties are likely to hide information:

• Much is at stake (money, custody, job, reputation, legal judgment).

• Truth is difficult to prove (no witnesses, no paper trail).

• Being found out is likely to have few consequences.

• One side has much more information than the other.

➤ Stipulate in the agreement to mediate, then again during the Opening, that they agree to share all relevant information (e.g., disclosure of assets and debts in a divorce mediation).

➤ Use Separate Conversations to get a better sense of whether parties are intentionally lying or withholding information.

8.5
WHEN THE "TRUTH" IS AN ISSUE

• *How would establishing the facts change things for you?*

• *This accusation seems to upset you more than anything else. Can you tell us why?*

In Separate Conversations:

• *Do you have further knowledge or documents that might influence the other party's decisions?*

• *Is there anything I as mediator need to know that you haven't yet decided to bring up at the table?*

Plain description of facts and needs

Filtering out emotions and interpretations

When you reflect back examples and impacts, use tactful wording that takes out the sting and the drama, but retains the kernel of facts and interests.

- **FACTS** = description of behaviors, how things are.

- **INTERESTS** = what the speaker seems to need or want.

Your goal is to be accurate and unbiased, so that the speaker nods, "Yes, that's what I'm saying," while the other participants are thinking, "Oh, that's what made her mad. Now I get it."

Filtering out the judgments and emotional charge will not change what people believe or feel. However, it *will* help them move forward by enabling them to talk about substance — the things they *can* change — without emotions about past problems dominating the conversation.

Context for examples on the following pages

➤ **Get enough information.** You may not always know enough to cleanly summarize or reframe what a participant is saying (or not saying). You may first need to listen for implied or missing information, then ask questions to reach an accurate and explicit understanding. The following five pages present reframing techniques you can use to draw more information from participants.

➤ **Reflect back to the speaker.** You don't want to explain one participant's views to the other parties, or put them on the spot. On the "Plain description" page which follows, assume that the mediator is looking at Mary, while (presumably) George listens.

➤ The mediators speak to all the participants together when describing a joint interest (*You all obviously care about X*) or when proposing topics for the Topic List.

Plain description of facts and needs

THE EMOTIONAL CHARGE	HOW TO FILTER IT OUT	MEDIATOR RESTATES FACTS AND NEEDS
JUDGMENTS "George is a slob. He's an embarrassment to the company."	Recognize the emotion they're trying to convey, then restate the description without the emotive language. Describe what someone DOES rather than how the person or the situation IS.	*So Mary, you're angry about the number of papers and other things George has around his desk?*
EXAGGERATIONS "George always dumps his piles of junk all over the floor."	Snip out generalization words (never, totally, everyone…), name the emotion that dramatic words imply.	*When George puts unorganized piles of paper on the floor, it really irritates you.*
LOADED WORDS "George has a hoarding problem!"	Avoid labels and ideas that echo one side's views.	*You think that George keeps a lot more things than is necessary.*
PERSONALIZING AND BLAME "If it weren't for George's rude and unprofessional piles of junk, I could make it through the day." "I feel disrespected by George's utter disregard of my needs."	Remove the other person's name. Restate the speaker's needs (interests) independent of the other person's cooperation. Do the same with "feeling talk" that is masking an accusation or judgment.	*Paper piles on the floor really bother you. You want your office space to reflect your professionalism, the high-quality work you do.* *So Mary, for you, keeping a shared office neat is a sign of respect and consideration.*
DEMANDS, THREATS "I don't want a single paper in sight. If I come in in the morning and find George has left stuff out, I'm going to shred it!"	Overlook the demands and threats. Instead, describe what underlying need it indicates. When possible, word it in a way that makes their interest sound like a reasonable one.	*You like to work in an office where papers are mostly put away out of sight at the end of the workday so you can have a clean start in the morning.*

Flip it! ➡ Outcome-focused interests

➤ Flip it! moves

In setting up interests for problem-solving, the mediator takes a participant's description of what they don't like about the past, and "flips" it to extrapolate what conditions the person probably wants in the future.

Negative ➡ Positive. Frame the interest as a benefit, a hope, as what people *can* have or do, rather than what they can't. Shift "oughts" to "wants," — describe what behavior would be helpful, rather than what the other person *should* (or shouldn't) do.

Past & present ➡ Desired future. Frame the interest as conditions they hope to create, rather than complaints they have about the past or present.

WHAT THEY DISLIKE	POSITIVE FUTURE INTEREST
"They owe me $8,500 in damages, but they're hiding behind technicalities in order not to pay."	*You need to recoup your costs, and want to feel that you are being treated fairly?*
"You never back me up! You overturn my discipline decisions whenever people come to complain. No wonder the employees ignore my authority!"	*You'd like Pete to back you up when you discipline an employee, and to know you are both on the same page?*
"Keesha ALWAYS leaves early, and I have to cover for her. I refuse to lie for her or to do her work anymore! Everyone here should pull their own weight."	*Sounds like you want to concentrate on taking care of your patients. When employees don't work a full shift, you'd like a fair policy for how that person's load is covered—is that it?*
"Just stop the name calling, the eye-rolling, and the rumors already!"	*When one of you is mad about something, you'd like to talk it over face to face before rumors and arguments get started?*
"Their crude comments during faculty meetings are offensive to me. It shouldn't be allowed."	*Sounds like you would like to have friendly, business-focused meetings.*

Tactful wording of interests and topics

When summarizing interests and topics, filter out emotions, judgments, and interpretations, just as you did with "plain descriptions" [**see pages 152–53**]. As much as possible, word interests and topics to be:

✓ **Outcome-focused**

✓ **Non-partisan**

✓ **Non-judgmental**

✓ **Reasonable**

	THEIR VIEW...	INTERESTS	TOPIC
OUTCOME-FOCUSED Doesn't just restate the problem. (See also "Flip it!" on the previous page.)	"The problem is Viola screaming and cursing at my kids."	*You want your kids to enjoy playing outside.* *You want your neighbors to treat your kids kindly.*	*How to improve the interaction between Marty's boys and Viola.*
NON-PARTISAN Uses neutral, inclusive words that do not echo one party's view. Describes the state they want, not how the other should behave or think.	"Her vicious dogs are out of control." "Marty's unsupervised boys throw stones at my dogs."	*You're both concerned about safety—Marty, for your boys, and Viola, for your dogs.*	*How to have safe interactions between the boys and the dogs so that neither get hurt.*
NON-JUDGMENTAL Does not judge persons, behaviors, choices, or beliefs.	"Marty doesn't supervise the boys—they are allowed to run wild."	*Viola, you'd like to be able to get in touch with Marty if you see a problem.*	*How to communicate when problems come up, especially when the boys are home and Marty is at work.*
REASONABLE The part of their concern which most people would consider reasonable, legitimate.	"I'm calling the animal control center to have those vicious dogs put down! "	*Marty, you want certainty that the dogs won't get loose from Viola's yard.*	*How to secure Viola's fence and gate.*

Summary of interests

POSITIONS AND INTERPRETATIONS	HOW THE MEDIATOR MIGHT SUMMARIZE THE PARTIES' INTERESTS
Russell says he will resign from the committee unless Walter apologizes for the untrue and nasty comments he made about Russell to key members of the church. Walter counters that Russell is high-handedly excluding him from financial decisions—and botching those decisions besides. Russell *should* resign. Walter says he isn't sorry and he won't apologize till hell freezes over.	**EMPHASIZING COMMON INTERESTS** *You have a common interest in finding the right pastor for your church, and you've worked very hard for a year on this committee. It sounds like both of you would like to see it through.* *So you're both concerned about personal reputation and being appreciated even when opinions differ. And you both want to be included in financial decisions, yes?*
Pat is asking the company to pay for evening and weekend daycare expenses. She made this a condition of accepting the promotion. The company should not be allowed to renege on its promises. Zach insists that they cannot pay because it is against the company policy of no perks. The VP never made any such promise. If Pat can't hack this promotion, she should go back to her old job.	**ONE SIDE, THEN THE OTHER SIDE'S INTERESTS** *As I understand it, Zach, you are pleased with Pat's work, and would like to keep her in this new position. And you are also concerned about the integrity of the company's "no favors" compensation policy. Is that right?* *And, Pat, you want to keep this job, but you need some financial assistance and some scheduling flexibility to handle the daycare situation. And you want to know that this company is treating you fairly. Did I summarize that accurately?*
Neighbors demand that a nearby movie theater control the teenaged crowds that gather there. They also want patrons to park at night in the shopping center lot across the street instead of in front of their houses and blocking their driveways. The theater owners say the town should be grateful that they keep the teenagers safely entertained. Unfortunately, they can't control their patrons once they leave the premises. The shopping center charges much higher access fees than the theater can afford. If neighbor harassment of them and their patrons doesn't stop, they will go to court.	**INTERESTS AS A SET OF CRITERIA** *After listening to what matters to you, it seems that a workable agreement has to meet these criteria:* ✓ *The residents need quiet between 10: 30 PM and 7:30 AM, and access to parking near their houses.* ✓ *The movie theater wants to make sure the number of patrons does not drop off.* ✓ *Solutions should preserve the friendly, safe neighborhood feeling—which everyone has agreed is good for the residents and the businesses.* *Does that sound right?*

Topic List examples

Creating the Topic List goes one step further than summarizing interests. The mediator sorts the parties' interests into groups and reframes them as joint problems for the parties to work through. [**See pages 59–62.**]

THEIR RAW COMPLAINTS ➡	EVENTUAL TOPIC LIST
"How dare you expect us to just rubber-stamp your decision! You talk to your buddies but ignore the rest of us. I won't be bulldozed into letting this budget pass until we've talked about each and every line." "Some people just can't deal with any change. No matter what we propose you always moan and roll your eyes but make no constructive suggestions. Furthermore you haven't done a lick of work for this committee for years except to throw sand in the gears."	*Since you've both decided to stay on this committee, these seem to be the main topics you need to talk through and resolve tonight:* ✓ ***Budget**—how the committee will make budget decisions.* ✓ ***Planning**—what role each of you will have in planning next year's program.* ✓ ***Communication and decision-making**—what you want to do next time differences arise within the committee.* *Do you have any additions or changes? Is the wording okay?*
"Don't you dare tell my kids you are going to smack them! You are the adult, control yourself! If you have a problem, you come to ME. Got it?" "Your kids are brats! They are completely un-disciplined. They push other kids, scratch and hit, and don't listen to adults who tell them to stop."	*You've both said you'd like a set of posted rules for parents. It sounds like there are two topics to discuss and decide:* ✓ *When & how should adults nearby intervene when it involves other people's kids?* ✓ *How to communicate with each other when problems with kids come up.* *Does this cover everything you need to discuss?*
"When you talk to me, I expect some respect. You are the secretary, not the manager around here. If I tell you to get this project in the mail, then that's what you're supposed to do. This half-assed job is unacceptable!" "You aren't my supervisor, *Jonah* is. *He* is the one who assigns my work, not you. I don't care if you have been here ten years and have a fancy title. Put your request in the in-box just like everyone else has to. Don't dump your work on me!"	*You have decided you want to work apart as much as possible, and agree on rules for when you interact. Would these topics cover it?* ✓ *Who assigns Trina's work.* ✓ *How to communicate about work tasks, schedules, quality of work.* ✓ *How you want to treat each other.* *Did I leave anything out?*

Eliciting ideas: Brainstorming

▶ Getting lots of ideas out

Brainstorming a cloud of ideas can produce breakthroughs, as well as lift the mood and get people cooperating. It gets the swirl of options and concerns out of people's heads, and up on the wall where they can take in the whole picture, and focus less on their own particular ideas.

Brainstorm guidelines

1. **Think freely about possibilities.** *Bring up anything that pops to mind, workable or not. We're looking for volume, not quality!*

2. **No commentary.** *You can add a variant of a previous idea, but hold back from "liking" or "rejecting" for the moment.*

3. **No commitment.** Explain that the goal is to scan widely for potentially useful ideas, not to put forward official proposals. *Raw ideas are welcome, even ones you aren't sure you agree with. Ideas should not be taken as negotiation proposals or as promises.*

Assisting

If participants seem to be having trouble thinking freely or putting their frank ideas out there, you might:

➤ Suggest that each person write several ideas on a sheet of paper, which you then collect and read aloud.

➤ Ask members of each party to brainstorm amongst themselves and then come back to the table.

➤ Ask questions or put out categories that jog new thoughts: *What are ways you might use scheduling to solve this?*

Eliciting ideas: Opening up possibilities

▶ Move them away from positions

Ways to help participants venture beyond their positions in coming up with options:

➤ **Ask an unexpected question**, one that frames the subject in a different way, so that they can't offer their standard answer as easily. The strategies on this page and the next can help you do that.

➤ **What can you offer?** (The opposite of "What do you want from them?") *Is there anything you might personally offer to do that will help resolve this issue?*

➤ **Two solutions.** Ask each party to present two distinctly different suggestions, either of which would be okay with them.

➤ **Think time.** Take quiet time for everyone to make their own list of possibilities. In some cases, you can request they do this before the mediation or between sessions.

▶ Zoom to the right level of specificity

Mediators zoom in to specifics and out to the bigger picture throughout the mediation. During the problem-solving phases, start by defining interests and topics broadly enough that several solutions are possible, but not so wide open as to be unmanageable [**page 148**]. Then zoom out to help parties evaluate options — does the idea work at the wider level as well as at the practical-implementation level?

➤ **Zoom out** to get to longer-term, overall solutions. Use this "wide angle" when they are hyper-focused on particulars ("You never say good morning to me.") or when fixing immediate problems won't change the root causes. (Even if they renegotiate the upcoming holiday work schedule, it might also be wise to look at how the scheduling *process* is working more generally.)

➤ **Zoom in** to get participants thinking more concretely about how their specific wishes and ideas would actually play out. If Faye says, "We should just talk to each other when there's a problem," but in the past she's slammed doors, zoom in to details — HOW and WHEN do they want to talk to each other?

**8.6
ZOOM-OUT
QUESTIONS**

- *What policy changes might clarify the situation, so you don't have to deal with this aggravation so often?*

- *What industries out there are dealing creatively with similar problems?*

- *What changes can you make today that will put your club in a good place two years down the road?*

**8.7
ZOOM IN QUESTIONS**

- *If you did decide to cancel the whole thing, what steps would you need to take? What other problems might come up?*

- *You say you don't want Joe left alone. What specific ideas do you have for how to make that work?*

- *Let's go through the calendar, week by week…*

Eliciting ideas: Opening up possibilities

▶ Use imagination

The following methods won't suit some types of mediation, but they can lighten the mood and break open people's habitual ways of thinking about their problems.

"Changing hats"

Ask everyone to put on a new "hat" for a minute. You can suggest one of Edward de Bono's classics (he invented this idea): seeking information, gut reaction, devil's advocate, optimist, creative. Or choose occupational hats: accountant, parent, journalist, administrative assistant, lawyer, nerd, banker, team sport player, dreamer, supervisor, pragmatist, warrior. *What options come to mind now?* You can also use this when they are testing out an idea: *How does this proposed option look when you put on the "mayor's hat"?*

Magic wands

➤ Imagine a fantasy situation where obstacles are magically removed:

> *If you could wave a wand and all budget limits disappeared, how would you solve this problem?*

> *Pretend your boss is on a 4-week trip to Antarctica. What might work if she wasn't around to disapprove?*

Visioning an ideal future scenario

1. Ask them to picture in detail how they want something to be.

2. Then have them think through the steps that are most likely to get them there.

Note: Don't try visioning an ideal future if they are still openly angry. ("The other person got fired, moved far away, and hasn't been seen since.")

What's working now?

If they've only been looking at problems, try a positive tack: What are they already doing that works and that they can they build on? Is there any project or topic that they can put energy into together, even if they still disagree about many other issues?

**8.8
VISIONING EXAMPLES**

• *It's one year from now. You're both still working for this department (still married, still living next door, still partners in this venture). What's the happiest scenario you can imagine?*

• *Imagine you have been working at your dream job for several months. You arrive at work whistling and open the door...what do you see? What conversations do you have? What tasks are you doing that day? Who are you working with, and what are those people doing?*

Can mediators suggest options?

This chapter is titled, "Solving the Problem." It really should read, "Guiding Their Problem-Solving Process." This distinction lies at the heart of the outcome-neutral mediator role presented in this book.

We strongly recommend that mediators avoid suggesting or critiquing options. Even in contexts where mediator-experts routinely evaluate the strength of each party's case, and recommend solutions, the parties may develop a stronger agreement and working relationship if mediators let them take the lead in developing and evaluating solutions.

▶ Reasons for holding back

➢ Working together on an agreement can build a more cooperative interaction and willingness to follow through. Even if you hand parties the perfect solution, you pre-empt that key experience and motivation.

➢ Participants are the real "experts." They know their context better than you do. And they are the ones who have to live with the results.

➢ When a solution is theirs, people have greater stake in making it work.

➢ If your idea seems wrong or unworkable to them, you risk seeming condescending or clueless. Worse, if only one party likes your idea, the other party may question your impartiality.

➢ If you hand them the solution, it can make them feel stupid, petty, or ungenerous for not having offered it themselves.

➢ Even if the mediator offers a tentative suggestion, the parties may feel it is impolite or impolitic to say no. Or they may defer to your authority.

➢ If the agreement falls apart later, whose fault will it be? —yours.

➢ What's your hurry? If they are stuck, it is rarely because they can't imagine workable solutions. More likely they are still mired in adversarial mode and not thinking clearly, or are stalling for strategic or emotional reasons.

▶ Information about *kinds* of options

If you see a **category** of solution that has not occurred to the parties, present it as information rather than as a suggestion.

➢ Describe how some other people who were in a similar situation had success with X. [**See sidebar.**]

➢ Use a hesitant, casual tone, almost shrugging off the idea.

8.9
PRESENTING KINDS OF OPTIONS

• *We've seen other companies solve this issue by hiring an outside service.*

• *There seem to be several directions you might take: revising the regulations, rewarding voluntary participation, and one you haven't mentioned yet— using monitoring technology.*

• *Would developing some sort of schedule be useful?*

Visual aids for making decisions

When there is a lot of information to take into account, or detailed options to compare, use visual aids. [**See page 132.**]

➤ Post a list of the interests they want to meet—a criteria checklist they can refer to throughout Reaching Resolution discussions.

➤ Work collectively with visual project-planning tools such as timelines and calendar grids, decision trees, task-flow charts, or comparison grids, such as the examples below.

Plusses and minuses: Comparing options

Ask each person to contribute something for each quadrant. In addition to helping them weigh different options, this tool can clarify the list of priority interests the agreement must meet. Give the options neutral labels like "A" and "B." Avoid calling them "Tom's idea" or "Jill's proposal."

OPTION A	OPTION B
List the + plusses here	List + plusses
List − minuses	List − minuses

Mapping out possible impact of Option X on each participant

	EXTRA HOURS PER WEEK	COSTS	RESPONSIBILITY?	IMPACT
MARTHA	+5	$12,000 this budget year	Collecting data, revising budget	Higher workload Less control over program implementation
JAMAL	+2	Lose assistant	Filing forms	Program less effective?
ACCOUNTING DEPT.	+1	$3,500/year	Whole system	Comply with new laws More oversight of programs

Types of resolution

When participants are having trouble setting goals for the mediation or imagining any resolution, or are deadlocked over options, you can outline some of these different types of resolution to broaden their thinking about what is possible. Example terms of agreement are in parentheses.

➤ **Tasks & behaviors.** Planning how they will address specific, substantive problems, down to the details: Who will do what, when, how. (Take charge of cleanup, return from lunch by 1pm, finish the project next month.)

➤ **Interactions.** Deciding how they will treat each other or work with each other. (Consult when a problem comes up, set up a weekly meeting, say hello when passing by.)

➤ **Restoring balance** for grievances, inequities, damages. (Acknowledge fault, pay for losses suffered, trade favors, stop rumors, compensate for trouble caused.)

➤ **Laying out priorities, principles.** ("We want each department to have input into this decision." "We value unscheduled family time and want to increase it." "We want newcomers to feel welcome.")

➤ **Deciding who will decide.** ("We'll have a membership vote." "Cynthia will make final decisions about publications." "We'll ask an engineer we both trust to inspect the building, and agree to follow that recommendation.")

➤ **Larger context.** Change the environment or the system. (Put up a fence, write a policy, reach out to organize with others experiencing similar conflicts, change the office layout, take political action.)

➤ **Starting with one joint project or activity** that is modest-sized and not controversial. This is a proven, effective way to (re)build relationships. It gives people an unselfconscious way to reconnect, and can nurture a cooperative spirit that may help them address more difficult issues later.

"Typical" or "good enough" resolutions

This may be mediation heresy, but it is not always possible or necessary to create fresh solutions, or to satisfy every interest. The parties may not be willing to spend the time and effort this can take, especially if they don't foresee interacting in the future.

In common types of disputes, creative options and legal precedents may be well-developed. Such pre-made solutions may offer a sensible way to reach an efficient and viable resolution, as long as the mediator still has the parties explore whether an uncommon solution might be a better fit for this particular situation.

Templates, model agreements

Parties can consult experts or search online to find sample agreements, templates, and best-practices guidelines, which can suggest what terms are generally considered fair and workable. (Be cautious about providing these yourself, so that you don't overstep into "unauthorized practice of law.") Review these together, line by line. Don't let them grant it too much authority—encourage them to adapt it to their needs and situation.

Trades, mutual concessions

What might parties each be willing to give up to get something they value more in return? First, help each party think through their priorities and possible consequences, so that they don't give anything up impulsively or under pressure.

Formulas

Formulas—such as splitting the difference or taking turns—can help parties decide something quickly in a way that feels objective and fair. "Jane will cut the pie; Dick gets to choose which piece he wants." In addition to formulas, parties can also agree to honor external standards, recommendations, or appraisals.

➤ **Is it really fair?** An "equal" distribution of resources or tasks may turn out to be neither fair nor workable.

➤ **Can they live with it?** Even if they agree on the formula, they also need to feel they can live with the resultant outcome.

➤ **Are they just tired?** People often resort to formulas when they're thinking, "OK, I'm done, let's just decide something and get out of here." That may be a smart judgment about what is worth their time. Or it may be that they just need a break or to sleep on it.

What-ifs

What-if scenarios help parties make sure they've prepared for unexpected or unwelcome events. After they've walked through possible changes and problems that could arise, they can decide which future contingencies are important to cover in their agreement. Note that we are not talking about the other kind of what-if questions which propose a solution (What if you just stayed home on Mondays?).

Scan for potential uncertainties

Ask what they worry might happen that could jeopardize part of the agreement, either in the short or the long term. Explore those what-if scenarios first. Then raise any others they've overlooked.

- **External support.** Does any aspect depend on other people or external organizations? If so, what if they disapprove, or are not as supportive or reliable as the parties expect?

- **Agreement terms no longer workable.** What if one party finds that part or all of the agreement is not doable or helpful anymore? Or that they occasionally need to bend it or break it?

- **Changes in resources.** What if someone finds themselves facing financial, health, or other unexpected troubles that make it hard to keep their promises?

- **Changes in the parties.** A participant may leave (their job, the neighborhood, etc.), or a new person come in. Is this agreement between institutions or between people? What if participating organizations go out of business, or want to withdraw? How will the parenting agreement work if an ex-partner remarries?

- **Environment changes.** What if the company's goals shift and new policies or practices come online? What might happen if the regulations are tightened?

If you think they are still denying likely consequences, say so:

> *I'm worried about this agreement holding up. Expecting kids who live next door to "never talk to each other" just doesn't seem realistic.*

> *Well, you all hope your boss will be glad to make this change, but let's think about a fallback option in case she says no. Otherwise, you may be back at square one.*

**8.10
SCANNING FOR
POTENTIAL
DIFFICULTIES**

- *What if you agree to this solution and _____ happens?*

- *Will this satisfy the requirements of your _____ (CEO, license, legal obligations…)? What will you do if it doesn't?*

- *What other complications might arise?*

Fallbacks: Contingencies, uncertainties

▶ Provide for contingencies

Once they've identified potential what-if problems, here are some ways to incorporate those uncertainties into an agreement:

➤ **If one party's actions depend on the other party's actions**, spell out what happens either way—What Regina agrees to do when Karl finishes X, and what she will do if X doesn't get done. Or de-link the actions and list them as separate promises. (Karl drafts the report. Regina talks to the donors.)

➤ **Safety nets.** When they're not sure they will be able to follow through, agree on how that will be handled:

> *If for any reason one of us can't meet this timeline, we will let each other know X days in advance _____ (talk about it, hire a temp, etc.).*

➤ **For areas where the future is too uncertain**, parties may wish to record only a general intent, to avoid being locked into something they may not be able to carry out:

> *We intend to schedule every ensemble for at least one performance next season, but will not be able to guarantee a slot until we have completed renovating the auditorium.*

▶ Fallbacks

➤ **Fallbacks are backup options** for when their chosen option doesn't work out—a Plan B.

➤ **Fallbacks can also prepare for several potential scenarios.** For example, if one parent is job-hunting, a custody agreement could attach a second schedule to be used in the event that the parent moves more than two hours away.

➤ **Spelling out the alternatives is safer** than "We agree to be flexible about who covers the lunch hour." In mediation, you can work with the parties to identify the most foreseeable changes, but leave it to them and to their lawyers how detailed they want their contingency plans to be, as lawyers are trained to comb through contingencies thoroughly and protect their clients from surprises.

BUT WHAT HAPPENS IF ... ?

elizabeth

Step-down agreements: Smaller scope

When participants struggle to reach agreement, but are still committed to forging some kind of resolution, consider a "step-down," an agreement that is less sturdy or final but still moves them towards their goals.

STRONGER AGREEMENT	STEP-DOWN
Agreement on actions	**Problem statement:** clarity about where parties disagree.
Agreement on actions	**Agreement in principle:** a general direction the parties would like to go, even if they're not yet sure how to make it happen.
Agreement on actions	**Priorities, principles:** guidelines for later activity or decisions.
Commitment to action	**Recommendations for action, voluntary compliance.**
Permanent	**Trial run or provisional:** agreement for a limited time, or an interim period, until other decisions or changes happen.
Comprehensive: covers all topics, all details.	**Partial** agreement, with or without commitment to work through the rest of the topics.
Unconditional: people will follow through no matter what else happens.	**Dependent:** Follow-through depends on the action of others, or external conditions.
Parties decide	**Experts or arbiters** asked to decide. Parties agree how they will be chosen.
Roots: agreement addresses larger causes, systems.	**Repair:** agreement fixes particular problems or symptoms.

When there's no agreement

▶ Partial agreement

If their hesitations about reaching an agreement grow more set during the Reaching Resolution phase, look for ways to record those sections of the agreement that have seemed to be mutually agreeable. Walking out empty-handed can harden the impression that the whole session was a waste of their time and that the other side is impossible to deal with.

> ➤ **Underscore any viable points of agreement**, and if appropriate ask whether they want to write those down, or record anything else that was resolved during the session.

> ➤ **See if they want to try** a temporary or smaller-scope agreement. [**See page 167.**]

▶ No agreement

If they have gotten this far and have reached an impasse, it can be hard for mediators to let go of their hopes for resolution. Worse, to justify to themselves their decision to walk away, people may quickly turn unkind. The party more willing to work something out can feel vulnerable — having talked candidly or offered to compromise, they are now facing an "enemy" who has more information to use against them and is probably going to use harsher methods to get what they want.

As mediator, try to swallow your disappointment and dismay. Concentrate on salvaging as much feeling of goodwill between them as you can. You want them to leave in a mood of respectful regret. Review "Is it time to quit?" [**See page 136.**]

> ➤ **Acknowledge that they are not able to resolve their dispute today.**

> ➤ **Discuss consequences and alternatives.** Talk with them individually or collectively about what they plan to do next.

> ➤ **Note their progress.** You hope they have learned from each other, that they now have a clearer idea of what they each want and need. Thank them for the time, attention, and best efforts they have invested.

Freedom of self-determination is at the heart of this model of mediation. If participants now have a clearer understanding of their situation and what they really want, then you have done useful work, even if sometimes their choices make you feel sad or inadequate.

Final review: Workability

Does the agreement as a whole seem workable? Suggest they review it with the following issues in mind, and adjust the terms as needed.

Resources

✓ **Authority:** Approval, access, part of job description, permission to implement, support of higher-ups.

✓ **Ability:** Skills, tools, knowledge, information.

✓ **Means:** Money, materials, equipment, time, people.

✓ **Motivation:** Do they have the energy to carry through?

Support

✓ How will they explain the agreement to others? What reactions do they expect?

✓ How can they elicit active support? Does the agreement need to be sweetened or reframed to persuade the wider institution or community to assist in implementing it?

✓ Are there fallback plans for any decisions which rely on others for support, permission, or implementation?

Legalities, rules, policies

✓ Does the agreement accord with the law and regulations? (A question the mediator should pose, but not answer.)

✓ Does it accord with internal policies and customary practices of their organizations?

✓ Are there aspects of the agreement which might raise legal challenges or spark further disagreements?

Broader sustainability

Disputes don't happen in isolation—they emerge and dissipate in the context of a company, a neighborhood, a family, a town, an organization.

> *How might this agreement impact or benefit your company (your town, your family, other parties experiencing similar issues)?*

> *The third point of agreement affects several other groups. What information or opportunity for input needs to be made available to them?*

Final review: Future

▶ Adjusting the agreement afterwards

Present the agreement as actions the participants promise to adhere to and not change unilaterally. If it isn't working or circumstances have changed, instead of getting angry about someone "breaking" the agreement, you want them to think, "Guess it's time to talk about adjusting the agreement." This can be more effective than trying to set up a system of sanctions and external enforcement.

> **Ask what process they want for handling unforeseen issues.**

> *If a problem comes up with this agreement, how would you like to communicate or make decisions about it?*

For example, they might agree to meet once a month, to communicate through a mutual friend, to submit reports to each other, or to meet with the mediator again.

> **How much discretion or flexibility are they willing to grant** the other party? (Record those boundaries though: "The results are due July 10 but no later than one week after that.")

▶ Agreement lifespan

> **How long should the agreement last?** Do they want an end point, a renewal date, or a periodic review? Or is it okay to simply let it fade away when it is no longer relevant?

> **Evaluating outcomes:** If they expect to change their agreement down the road, or need to report results, they may also want to set up a means for evaluation. The more specific the agreement (who, where, when, how much), the easier it is to evaluate the outcomes.

▶ Bringing their best hopes into being

At its best, an agreement "sets things right" and prepares for a more positive climate. Review in your own mind, if not out loud, how well this agreement supports the parties in:

✓ **(Re)building their relationship.**

✓ **Tying up all loose ends,** particularly if future interaction is unlikely.

✓ **Lessening their burdens and stress,** on balance, even if promised actions require effort and expense.

Sample agreements

Landlord/Tenant

- Parker James agrees that he will look for another apartment and be out by November 30.

- Mariana DiPietro agrees the cat can stay till then.

- Parker agrees to keep the cat inside the apartment.

- Mariana agrees to ask neighbors to speak directly to Parker if they have a problem with the cat.

- Mariana agrees to give Parker a good reference to other landlords or apartment managers.

- Both agree that, for the remaining three months, they will communicate by leaving notes in the mailbox.

- Both agree that, when Parker moves out, they will walk through the apartment together to assess any cleaning or damages to be subtracted from the deposit, as listed in the lease.

Family (Elder/Siblings)

- Henry/Granddaddy agrees that he needs to move to a facility. He wants to have his own room and a place to garden.

- Everyone agrees that this should happen by early September. Kurt and Danielle agree that Granddaddy can stay with them for up to eight weeks if there is a delay in finding him a place.

- Everyone agrees that Timmy should handle the sale of the condo. Timmy agrees to consult with Kurt and Bob about pricing decisions and get their approval in writing before accepting the final offer. If they cannot agree, the three brothers agree to meet with the mediators again.

- Bob agrees to check with Henrietta about taking the parrot.

- Jeanne agrees to see that the condo gets cleaned out.

- Each person agrees to put two full days into cleanup, to be negotiated with Jeanne.

Sample agreements

Organization leadership

July 19 Interim Agreement

Jorge M., Katherine C., and Markus J. met for two hours and discussed the roots of their differences over direction for the GoodWorks organization. We also shared our feelings about various incidents. We agreed to continue this conversation, and reached the following points of agreement:

- We agree that we will not talk to anyone in the organization about what was discussed today, and will only tell people, "We're making progress."

- We agree to be open with each other and with the Board about our differences in philosophy to encourage more open debate within the organization. We also want to bring to the Board the goals they *share* for GoodWorks' future.

- All three of us agree to be careful to uphold each other's reputations. Specifically, we agree to criticize viewpoints, not personalities or motivations.

- All agree that the Board needs to review mission and strategy, preferably with an outside facilitator. Perhaps an ongoing committee or a retreat? We will meet again August 3 to discuss this further.

Small business-to-business

Both Morgan and Tom expressed regret that this situation got out of hand.

1. Tom agrees that Tom's Toys will pay Gerry $5,400 by bank check before the end of this month. (This is $800 lower than the original fee to account for the lights that Tom replaced afterward.)

2. Morgan agrees that $5,400 will constitute full payment for his work, and the warranty will last 18 months.

3. Both agree to speak well or neutrally about each other's businesses.

Scenarios: problem-solving challenges

▶ Getting at the truth

➤ *Vivian, can we save your box of evidence details for later? First I want everyone to hear what's been happening and how it has affected you.*

➤ Glance through the evidence politely if she brings it out again in the Exchange, and ask her if there are one or two things she most wants to share with the Wileys. Ask Vivian questions about her evidence that get her talking to the other participants. Looking at a few photos can be helpful as everyone tries to explain them to you.

➤ Comment that people nearly always have different memories of significant events; this is normal. That even if they think the other person is plain wrong, it can be useful to find out what that person believes, to get an idea of where the other party is coming from.

➤ *You have a great chance today to plan how things will be from now on, without other people dictating that to you. Even if you still disagree about who did what to whom, maybe we can look at how to improve things so you don't dread going into work every morning.*

[**See pages 43, 151.**]

8.11
SCENARIO: GETTING AT THE TRUTH

Vivian starts the Listening go-round by taking out sheaves of evidence and a stack of photos she's taken of the Wileys' property. They accuse her of spying and completely misunderstanding their actions.

▶ No intention of resolving

➤ If you sense Mr. Berg is not participating in good faith, have a Separate Conversation. Give a plain description of what you observed, being careful to be supportive and nonjudgmental. *Each time the RoseWorks Company has agreed to your requests, you have told them it isn't enough and raised new concerns.*

➤ Check out what's on his mind: *What would make this mediation worth your time? What would it take for you to resolve the situation today?*

➤ Explore his options: *Is getting an agreement today important to you, or are you thinking you'd be better off letting the judge decide?*

➤ *Based on what we've discussed, what do you want to tell RoseWorks when we go back to the table?*

➤ You may want to end the mediation if the dynamic doesn't change.

8.12
SCENARIO: NO INTENTION OF RESOLVING

The mediators both suspect that RoseWorks Inc.'s landlord, Mr. Berg, has no intention of reaching an agreement and is looking forward to his day in court.

Scenarios: problem-solving challenges

Dug in

8.13
SCENARIO: DUG IN

What can we do with One-Note-Charlie? It doesn't matter what anyone else says or suggests, he just puts forth exactly the same demand over and over, that he wants full payment NOW for the work he's completed, and to be released from the contract. Period.

➤ Use Charlie's line-in-the-sand demand to explore interests. *Charlie, what has been the impact of not getting paid? If Harriet paid $4,500 today, how would that affect you? If you accepted her $3,000 offer? If she doesn't pay you anything?* (He may be more frank in a Separate Conversation.)

➤ Propose shifting gears to some topic for which Charlie does not already have a set answer. If they can get somewhere with the new topic, he may shift into more cooperative mode and become more flexible or creative about payments.

In Separate Conversations

➤ Ask what Charlie hopes to accomplish, what the best outcome of the mediation could be. Then discuss with him how he can get there.

➤ Acknowledge what Charlie is trying to achieve. *Charlie, you sound really frustrated. Seems like you've been repeating yourself for the last hour, but it hasn't changed Harriet's mind. Let's look at your options here.*

➤ *Do you think you'll convince Harriet to pay you fully today? OK, so let's assume you're going to continue to disagree. Where do we go from here?*

➤ What does he stand to lose if he agrees to settle? Speak to whatever fear, need to maintain face, or desire to walk away that you think may be motivating Charlie to dig in his heels.

> *Charlie, are you concerned that if you give an inch on this issue, other customers may hear the story and ask you to do more for less money?*

➤ Talk to Harriet privately about how she might change her approach or at least let Charlie know she heard what he said, so that Charlie may not feel the need to defend his position.

GOING FURTHER

THE TOOLBOX

9

Going further

▶ Training, adapting, evaluating

The contents of a book can only give a pale reflection of real-life observation and practice. We urge you to attend a mediation training program and to apprentice with an experienced mediator. Either accompany them or invite them to partner with you in your own setting.

With any craft, it is usually wise to train in one school, then from that secure starting point, venture out to learn other approaches. In this chapter we offer some thoughts on adapting the process and skills for different contexts, and give some pointers for several common adaptations — mediating informally, mediating with families, with children and teens, and between employees. Then we discuss evaluation, which is integral to adapting and refining your practice. The chapter concludes with information about this book's authors and contributors.

▶ Mediating where you are

Unofficial mediation

Like many readers of this book, you may mediate informally within the context of your work, your volunteer organization or religious community, or your local government — or for your friends, roommates, or family members. The process can be shaped to suit the situation. Even if you don't call it "mediation," you will still need to think through your role and make sure people genuinely accept your intervention:

➤ Know where the line is between impartial mediation and partisan advocacy, and between mediating and being one of the parties.

➤ Be clear with everyone what influence you will have over decisions.

➤ Be especially careful about confidentiality, and what notes you keep.

Specialized mediation

There are dozens of mediation sub-specialties, some with their own credentialing. Though we can't cover those here, we hope you will first absorb the process in this book and use it for a while before seeking out specialist training. Such courses are often strong on teaching information, light on practicing mediation fundamentals.

If you already have a specialty, by all means experiment with how mediation fits into your work. You are more likely to get mediation work if you combine mediation skills with your professional knowledge and networks — as teacher, contractor, lawyer, therapist, manager, politician, etc.

Adapting the process

9.1
SOME CULTURAL ASPECTS OF MEDIATION MODELS

- What venue is used

- Timing, duration

- What expression of emotion is appropriate, desirable

- Whose language

- Story-telling vs. abstract and future thinking

- How people are expected to behave at the mediation, and with each other

- Equality vs. hierarchy and status. Who gets respect. Who gets to speak, to decide

- What honor, respect, professionalism look like

- Beliefs about conflict. Why it happens, who should resolve it, and how

- Focus—task or people, goal or process

- Seeking harmony vs. seeking fairness

At a micro level, mediators adapt and experiment in every mediation as they respond to the moment. Techniques and process are secondary; do whatever helps the parties meet their needs and goals, and still follows your mediation principles and ethics.

Everything we recommend in this book is a jump-start for you to build a mediation approach that suits you and your context. That said, there's a benefit to following this handbook's process and methods for several mediations before you start adapting—it can take a while to get used to a new way of doing things and see the wisdom of it, especially if you have been trained in other professions.

When you are ready to experiment, work through the following three aspects of your mediation as you think about how to adapt what you do.

Understand your participants' context and culture

What do the kind of people you work with seem to expect and need out of mediation? How well do they understand your mediation process and how to participate in it? Observe what seems natural to them, what seems alien or confusing. Where is the greatest gap between what you hope they will understand or do and what actually happens?

Be self-aware, observe how you mediate now

Articulate your mediation principles. What change in the world do you hope your mediations will bring? What guidelines do you follow in deciding your role, your facilitation choices? Note what kind of participants irritate you, who you tend to favor and how. Identify your habits, preferred techniques, and which mode you rely on most—supporting, facilitating, or problem-solving. When might these habits lessen your ability to approach a situation with fresh awareness and flexibility?

Notice the strengths and biases of your mediation model

Every mediation model is rooted in particular values, assumptions, techniques, and cultural patterns. Who participates more easily in your model? Who might be at a disadvantage? For example, in ours, articulate people may do better for themselves, as may those who believe individuals can and should fix their own problems.

See the sidebar for aspects of cultural perspectives and practices embedded in every mediation, and the **mediatorshandbook.com** website for several pages discussing this topic.

Mediating with children & teens

Children and teenagers participate in mediation in family and community settings as well as in school. They usually catch on very quickly.

Some schools train students to mediate for each other. Older teens can make an effective team with an adult mediator for intergenerational conflicts. Consider training some young mediators to work with you!

▶ Relating to young participants

It can come as a surprise to young people when they are treated as equal participants in the conversation. The mediator wants to hear their story and their opinion. You are not acting like a teacher, a parent, or a judge, not telling the kids how they should think or behave.

➤ **Focus on the content of what they say, rather than on their youth.**

➤ **Use a kind and serious tone.** Do not try to be someone you're not in an attempt to build rapport.

➤ **No teaching, no preaching.** It brands you as just another adult.

➤ **No pressure.** Be careful not to use the mediation as a tool to make teens conform to adults' wishes.

➤ **Don't expect eye contact** or polite speech. Younger children may come in and out of the mediation rather than sit through.

➤ **Be careful not to undermine a parent's authority,** even if you disapprove of their approach. This can pose a delicate challenge, because young participants need to have their own voice in the discussion, and be able to trust you to support them.

▶ Structuring the mediation

➤ **Let them talk among themselves.** Once young participants are in cooperative mode, they may be more productive without you. Ask if they want to talk by themselves, and if so, set them up with a Topic List, worded as questions. Either sit at a distance, or let them know where they can find you, and check in every 10 minutes or so.

➤ **Teens in the throes of a group dispute** can completely override mediators who parachute in for a session, acting like "one more adult come to get us to behave." Teens, like adults, respond well to mediators who treat them with respect and speak to their interests. Build connections with the individual teens beforehand. Work together to design a session that feels like "theirs," and keep the number of participants small.

> **9.2**
> **SOME USEFUL TRANSLATIONS**
>
> - Listening to each perspective = Taking turns, telling what happened
>
> - Exchange = Talking it out
>
> - Meeting interests = Being fair to everybody
>
> - Agreement = What you all promise to do

Mediating across generations

▶ Young participants in conflict with adults

As with any mediation involving a significant power imbalance, mediators need to pay extra attention to promoting full participation when some of the participants are young.

➤ **Decisions.** Be clear from the beginning about how much say children or teens will have in the agreement. Will the adults make the final decision or have veto power? It can be disillusioning to participate in reaching resolutions, only to be overruled by an adult in the end.

➤ **Talk to children or teen participants in advance**, not just to their parents or teachers.

➤ **Divide your gaze and attention equally among all the participants.** You don't want the younger ones to feel all adult eyes upon them; neither do you want the adults to converse as if they weren't there.

➤ **Directly invite the young participants to speak** throughout the mediation, so they don't have to "interrupt" the adults. Also do this right away whenever an adult starts to speak *for* a child or teen.

➤ **Listening go-rounds.** Use prompts and questions if that helps draw out young participants' needs and experiences. You may also want to invite all of them to speak before the adults take their turns.

▶ Mediating with elderly participants

Mediation is an excellent option for families arguing over how to care for an aging family member. Specific training in so-called "eldercare" mediation is essential before you take this on, as the financial, psychological, familial, and legal aspects can be complex.

If an elderly person is simply one of the participants in an ordinary (non-eldercare) dispute, here are some mediation tips:

➤ **Plan in advance how to include elderly participants** in the conversation and decision-making, even if they have emotional and mental challenges. This includes choosing a good time and location.

➤ **Accessibility.** Review tips on pace, hearing difficulties, ways to help people follow the conversation and contribute to it. [**See pages 107–08, 118–19.**]

➤ **If relevant, make sure that the elder has informed advocacy**—lawyer, counselor, doctor, accountant—to represent their interests.

➤ **Be extra kind.** Many elder mediations are about coping with losses. A tender touch is often appreciated.

9.3
FAMILY SITUATIONS RIPE FOR MEDIATION

- Paul's second wife says either his teenage children move out or she and their toddler will leave.

- Ramon refuses to come to family events because his brother Elias will be there.

- Sonya is trying to get her two sisters to stop fighting about selling the old family home.

- Uncle Jack has asked for yet another loan.

- Alberto and June's marriage is strained by arguments about debts and spending.

- Family-owned WackyWidgets, Inc. is embroiled in a generational dispute about succession and equity.

- Anya and her kids have moved in with her mom. They are constantly arguing about housework, money, and childcare.

Mediating family conflicts

Complicated, intense, and ongoing, family conflicts are rarely easy to mediate, yet they can be deeply satisfying.

Caution: Do not attempt to mediate divorce, custody or eldercare issues, unless you are trained to do so.

For conflicts in your own family, recognize that you can't be fully impartial or outcome-neutral. Mediate only if everyone is glad to have you take that role.

▶ Facilitating family discussions

➤ **Work with a second mediator,** and anticipate several sessions.

➤ **Limit the scope.** Every family has a large supply of past hurts and current problems. Help them agree on a limited goal for the mediation. Which topics will most help them feel better about each other? Which will most help with making pressing decisions?

➤ **Reaffirm the family members' shared identity,** principles, goals, and interests, as long as you are sure there is real agreement about those.

> *I know you each care about what happens to your brother. Shall we start with a brief prayer for his well-being and the family's?*

> *You've all said that you're committed to reaching a decision that every family member feels comfortable with.*

➤ **Emphasize listening for anything NEW that they hear.** Throughout the session, ask people to report what new things they have heard or realized.

➤ **Let each person speak for themselves.** Whenever participants start to blame, speak for others, or comment about character and motives, return the conversation to examples and personal impact.

➤ **Give them a way to absorb hurtful information** and accusations. Do people need space to recompose themselves? Protection? A caring silence, a break, or a change of subject can be useful.

➤ **Give them openings to appreciate each other.** *What is one thing you like about sharing the house? What were some things you all enjoyed growing up?*

➤ **Counteract patterns of overlooking or blaming** certain family members. Bring attention to ignored statements. Reframe complaints and putdowns as a mutual topic of concern.

181

Mediating employee conflicts

Organizational politics — the struggle for influence, success, resources, security, and respect — flourish everywhere. Chances are, your mediation skills will prove useful again and again.

Careful set-up

Follow the process in the "Getting to the Table" chapter. Define your role, talk to each party in advance, and work out who should attend. If you are mediating within your own organization, check "Should I be the mediator?" [**See page 24.**] In addition:

✓ **Voluntary participation.** If a manager is arranging a mediation between employees, have them ask each party, *Call this mediator I'm considering and see if you think they might be helpful in the situation.* You don't want to be seen as the boss's stand-in or spy.

✓ **Risks.** Might participation potentially diminish one party's authority or put someone's job at risk? How can you structure the mediation to make this less likely?

✓ **Expectations.** Discuss — with the manager and/or participants — duration, cost, and expectations about outcome and for reporting back.

✓ **Decisions.** What decisions do the people at the table have the authority to make, and how much latitude do they have?

✓ **Scope.** Be clear about what mediation can and cannot change. To tackle conflicts that involve more than a handful of people, you'll need methods and knowledge beyond this book's scope.

Interpersonal aspects

➤ **Separate business goals and tasks from interpersonal tensions.** In workplace settings, people's first responsibility is to get work done well. A depersonalized agreement about the external context — purpose, processes, tasks — can make interpersonal interactions more structured, and therefore potentially less irritating and less disruptive.

➤ **If one participant or group is cast as the "problem,"** reframe complaints about them as a problem involving everyone. In the Options phase, ask how each person can help make the *other* person's job as successful as possible.

➤ **Be hypersensitive to participants' needs for confidentiality and face-saving** — maintaining their reputation within the organization, and their desire for autonomy and authority on the job.

Mediating employee conflicts

Use a systems approach

It's critical to concentrate on what's happening systemically. Even if the participants think they have a "personality conflict," there are sure to be organizational problems creating or fueling the dispute. Zero in on the places where there is lack of clarity or outright disagreement about roles, goals, and decisions:

➤ Where is there ambiguity? Disagreement about boundaries?

➤ What is each side's role? Which pieces of the work belong to each of them?

➤ Who has access to what information? Where does communication break down?

➤ How are decisions made and by whom? Who has the formal authority to make decisions about contested topics?

Key areas to discuss and decide

➤ **Formal vs. actual way things are done.** What are the official policies, processes, job descriptions, principles, etc.? (They may have to go dig to find out.) Where does their current reality diverge from that? What is contested?

➤ **How to bring formal and actual more in line with each other.** For example, they could recommend that management alter a policy, revise job descriptions, reconfirm lines of authority, or provide training.

➤ **What they can decide today.** What's interpersonal, or can be decided without involving others?

➤ **What goes back to the organization** for discussion and decisions?

9.4
GOAL- & TASK-ORIENTED CONVERSATION

Common goals & principles

- *You are both committed to giving the best, most humane health care to your patients that you can.*

- *This has been a good partnership, and your company would like to explore ways to continue that collaboration.*

Potential cooperation

- *Are there any tasks, however small, where you might be able to work together?*

- *What is going well now, and how can you build on that?*

© 2012 Jennifer E. Beer and Caroline C. Packard

Participant evaluation

No matter what type of mediations you are doing, two evaluation forms are essential: your assessment of the mediation session(s), and your self-evaluation. For formal mediations, you'll also need a participants' evaluation form. See **mediatorshandbook.com** for links to well-crafted forms from various programs that can serve as templates.

▶ Participant evaluations

You'll get more data if participants fill out an evaluation form at the close of mediation (perhaps to put in a sealed envelope), though some will appreciate the option of mailing it later or doing it online. Evaluations solicited some time after a mediation will reflect what has happened in the interim, which of course is valuable data, too.

First, decide what your goal is

Keep it brief enough that tired participants give you useful responses. This means you're unlikely to cover all of the potential goals below, so choose what's most important:

➤ Feedback and information to improve your mediation program, including any quality-control measures of mediator performance.

➤ Feedback for the mediators.

➤ Statistics to use in getting clients or grants. (76% of our mediations end with agreements, 88% say the mediation was helpful.)

➤ Giving the parties a chance to say what they think and feel. Maybe also to foster a positive, reflective attitude towards the experience.

Aspects you might assess

✓ How prepared they felt, how well logistics worked.

✓ How they experienced the mediator(s): how even-handed, fair, supportive, respectful, listening, understanding, etc.

✓ Their participation: Were they able to speak, to be heard, to decide?

✓ Mediator skill: getting people beyond tense moments or impasse on a topic, keeping things moving, giving everyone a turn, etc.

✓ Outcome: Was the conversation helpful? Was the agreement fair? Realistic? Did it answer their main concerns?

✓ Relationship: Has understanding increased? Will interactions be easier?

Mediator evaluation of a mediation

▶ Tracking trends, ideas, difficulties

Session evaluations are useful for mediation programs and practitioners to monitor trends and spot difficulties. Consider keeping names and identifying details out of the evaluation form, and de-linking it from records about the particular case. This allows mediators to discuss difficulties without violating promised confidentiality.

Data collection & practical aspects you might assess

➤ **Data:** Number of participants. Who mediated. Number and length of sessions. How much mediator/program time was spent before and between sessions. The type of dispute and the main issues. Their agreement: full, partial, written, verbal, none, not needed.

➤ **Logistics:** Any problems with scheduling, facilities, materials.

➤ **Preparation:** Were the "right" parties present, background information sufficient for mediators? Were participants' expectations and preparations appropriate?

➤ **Follow-up alerts** about anything else mediators or staff need to do.

▶ Reflecting on the mediation

These sample questions lend themselves to open-ended comments rather than measurement. Elicit observations rather than good/bad evaluation, as that tends to provide more information and learning.

✓ Did anything unusual happen?

✓ Did the standard process work, and if not, how did you change it?

✓ What strategies seemed to work?

✓ If you could do it over, what changes might you make?

✓ How do you judge the quality of their outcome/agreement?

✓ Did you use Separate Conversations, and were they helpful?

✓ How did you share the facilitation with your co-mediator?

✓ What did you learn from this mediation?

✓ Did it raise any significant issues that other mediators or the program might discuss further?

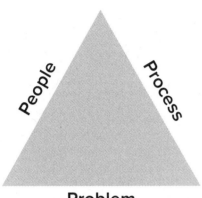

People / Process / Problem

Evaluating yourself

▶ Overall reflections on your mediating

1. List two or three things you did well. (It's good to start with this since most of us head for negatives right away.)

2. How did you respond to particular challenges in this mediation?

3. Where on the mediation triangle did most of your mediating efforts go?

4. What one thing did you learn about mediating?

5. What one thing do you want to pay attention to or try out next time?

▶ Some skills you may want to assess

Choose about six to eight behaviors you'd especially like to track, and stick to those for a while. For a form used by many mediators, select those behaviors that have greatest impact or are hardest to do well. Some perennials :

✓ Listening. Getting them talking, preferably to each other.

✓ Keeping focus on what's relevant, what's new, what moves parties forward to their goals.

✓ Being impartial yet showing empathy.

✓ Making sure everyone participates fully.

✓ Building a cooperative atmosphere, preventing escalation of hostility.

✓ Identifying and summarizing interests.

✓ Pacing, including bringing things to a close.

✓ Creating an effective Topic List and getting several options for each.

✓ Holding back on advice, moralizing, suggestions, opinions.

✓ Helping them think for themselves rather than explaining or persuading or asking lots of questions.

✓ Letting them do most of the work, and all of the deciding.

Note which skills you used, and what the effect was. Again, you will probably learn more (and scold yourself less) if you concentrate on describing how you responded to their behavior and how they in turn responded to you, rather than on "grading" your performance.

The *Handbook* "soup pot"

The Mediator's Handbook is a collaborative project which, like a soup simmering on the back of the stove, owes its rich flavor to many cooks, not just to the handfuls of spice and fresh vegetables thrown in shortly before serving.

For many years the *Handbook* was a publication of Friends Conflict Resolution Programs (FCRP). Eileen Stief started its mediation program in 1976. She and her volunteers developed our original mediation process by taking on disputes and experimenting with what worked. Whenever subsequent generations of mediators got too set on "how mediation is supposed to be done," Eileen would remind them, "We just made it up!" We hope our readers will also experiment in this spirit and not lock themselves into one "right" way to mediate.

Because there was no other mediation manual available to the general public at the time, intern Jenny Beer created the first *Mediator's Handbook* in 1982, guided by the wisdom and wit of staff member Charles Walker, who helped ground our mediation practice in Quaker principles of *active* nonviolence. She has been the chief writer of every edition since.

Subsequent staff members Sandi Adams, Chel Avery, Keelin Barry, Joan Broadfield, and Caroline Packard each brought passion and intellectual vigor to FCRP's mediation and training work, and greatly improved each iteration of the *Handbook*. It sold steadily, and in 1997, New Society Publishers agreed to publish the 3rd edition for a wider audience.

For the ground-up rewrite which is this 4th edition, Caroline Packard, Joan Broadfield, and Jenny Beer met regularly for two years, slicing and dicing, pondering "what is it we really do?" Caroline brought her keen analytic and synthetic intelligence to bear on every aspect of the process, added many new concepts and tools, and gave greater precision, clarity, and nuance to old ones. Joan brought wisdom and skill from her decades of mediation and anti-racism work to keep our content and process on an even keel. Meanwhile Jenny wrote, sketched, tore up, and wrote again.

We have also benefited from decades of absorbing the work of other practitioners, academics, trainers, and colleagues in wide-ranging fields. For an account of those who have influenced us the most, and who may in turn inspire you, please see the resources and recommendations at **mediatorshandbook.com.**

We hope that our readers will find value in the collective knowledge gathered in *The Mediator's Handbook* — our long-simmering pot of soup — and add their own seasonings as they gain mediation experience.

9.5 QUAKER ROOTS

- Belief in the equality of persons and in their capacity to listen, to speak truth as they see it, to change.

- A deep well of experience in consensus decision processes.

- The desire to see people build a just community through control of their own lives.

- The emphasis on learning through experience, rather than just accepting things on authority.

- The commitment not just to renounce violence, but to invent practical alternatives people can and will use.

Authors & contributors

9.6
BIBLIOGRAPHY & RESOURCES

mediatorshandbook.com also maintains an updated section to connect our readers with further resources:

- Bibliography: A selected list of works on mediation, conflict resolution, facilitation.

- Online resources: Annotated links to key organizations, websites, blogs. Also links to templates for mediation forms, and to information on mediation sub-specialities.

Authors

Jennifer E. Beer, PhD, has been chief writer and editor for all the editions of this *Handbook* and also authored *Peacemaking in Your Neighborhood*. She combines her mediation career and her training in cultural anthropology to teach negotiation at Wharton (University of Pennsylvania) and to lead workshops on mediation, negotiation, training design, and cross-cultural communication. As an independent consultant, Jenny also mediates organizational conflicts, facilitates meetings, and still volunteers as a community mediator.

Caroline C. Packard, JD, led Friends Conflict Resolution Programs for 15 years, and has trained many hundreds of mediators. An organizational change- and conflict-resolution specialist with 30 years' experience, she is a *cum laude* graduate of Yale College and NYU School of Law and a former corporate litigator with extensive formal training in psychology and organizational-systems analysis. Her research interest is in the evolutionary psychology of cooperation and conflict in groups. Caroline provides conflict-resolution services and training to organizations, professional partnerships, and families.

Contributors

Eileen Stief, MS, developed the original mediation process and core principles documented in the *Handbook*. After her years running Philadelphia Yearly Meeting's pilot program (today's Center for Resolutions), she worked in an environmental mediation consultancy. A gifted trainer, she taught a whole generation of mediators to work with community, multi-party, and environmental disputes.

Joan Broadfield has been a member of Philadelphia Yearly Meeting's conflict resolution and mediation programs since the beginning, serving on oversight committees and participating in innumerable projects. She and her late husband Ed, also a faithful mediator, have dedicated their lives to undoing racism and to practical methods for building peace. We cannot thank Joan enough for giving selflessly of her time, her mediating presence, her ideas, and her editing skills.

Acknowledgments. Caroline is especially grateful to her "root teachers," such as Rosa Packard, Edward Packard, Gabriel Rocco, Ira Roseman, Yvonne Agazarian and Rebecca Brand—and to her children, Amy and David, for making it all worthwhile! Jenny thanks colleagues William Kaplan, Bill Withers, Barbara Simmons, and Richard Shell for the excellent work they do in the world, and for opening up ideas and opportunities, and Elizabeth Nicholson and Michael Beer for wise advice and much appreciated support.

Organizational support

New Society Publishers

For the *Handbook's* longevity, we owe heartfelt thanks to New Society Publishers, which has faithfully kept it easily available to a wide audience for many years. And we are deeply grateful for the yeoman work Ingrid Witvoet and her team have invested and their patient—very patient—labors over this new edition.

Center for Resolutions

Elizabeth Elwood Gates, our cartoonist, graciously agreed to draw the delicious light notes for the *Handbook* in loving memory of her aunt Anne Richan. Anne poured her heart into community mediation, turning the Philadelphia Yearly Meeting's pilot program into an independent non-profit. Today called the Center for Resolutions, it serves Delaware County, PA, and beyond.

Brenda Wolfer, long-time director of the Center's mediation and training programs, has often given us feedback direct from the front lines. Over the decades, she and her colleagues have given us many opportunities to mediate, to train, and to experiment with new ideas. Thank you, and enjoy your richly earned retirement!

Philadelphia Yearly Meeting

For helping us publish this and many past editions, we thank the Philadelphia Yearly Meeting of the Religious Society of Friends. They provided the framework, the staff, the opportunities, and the funding for our Quaker ventures into mediation and training. They directly financed many incarnations of the *Handbook*. Additional funding for previous editions came from the Bequests Committee of Philadelphia Yearly Meeting, the Chace Fund, the Rice Family Foundation, and the Thomas H. and Mary Williams Shoemaker Fund.

Though this edition marks the end of Philadelphia Yearly Meeting's ownership, Friends' ideas and practices remain our foundation. This is our heritage, and we hope this book will continue to honor those visions and commitments while serving as a useful guide to mediators of all persuasions.

Index

If you have enjoyed *The Mediator's Handbook* you might also enjoy other

BOOKS TO BUILD A NEW SOCIETY

Our books provide positive solutions for people who want to
make a difference. We specialize in:

**Sustainable Living • Green Building • Peak Oil • Renewable Energy
Environment & Economy • Natural Building & Appropriate Technology
Progressive Leadership • Resistance and Community
Educational & Parenting Resources**

New Society Publishers

ENVIRONMENTAL BENEFITS STATEMENT

New Society Publishers has chosen to produce this book on recycled paper made with
100% post consumer waste, processed chlorine free, and old growth free.

For every 5,000 books printed, New Society saves the following resources:[1]

47	Trees
4,262	Pounds of Solid Waste
4,690	Gallons of Water
6,117	Kilowatt Hours of Electricity
7,748	Pounds of Greenhouse Gases
33	Pounds of HAPs, VOCs, and AOX Combined
12	Cubic Yards of Landfill Space

[1]Environmental benefits are calculated based on research done by the Environmental Defense Fund and other members of the Paper Task Force who study the environmental impacts of the paper industry.

For a full list of NSP's titles, please call 1-800-567-6772 *or check out our website at:*

www.newsociety.com